# Aging in Places

## About the Cover

The image "Bear with Hand," on the cover of this book, has been used with the permission of the revered artist, Harriet Johns. Harriet, who herself is aging, has lived much of her life in the American Southwest. Her artwork ranges from huge foundry-produced enamels to small prints, which together represent a wide range of subjects and styles, all with rich symbolism and vibrant colorations. The cover image comes from her Bear series. Harriet's bears hover in vast spaces in which they appear to be searching for something unknown. Bears are powerful symbols of courage and tenacity and, for me, they represent the dignified strength that we must all have as we travel through our own aging years.

# Aging in Places

## Reflective Preparation for the Future

Marian Leah Knapp, Ph.D.

Credits

Editor: Laurel J. Kayne

Proofreader: Pauline Chin

Graphic Design: David G. O'Neil


Published by

Loagy Bay Press

Chestnut Hill, Massachusetts


Printed in the United States of America


ISBN: 978-0-9895470-0-0

*For my parents*
*Anne and Louis Noah Gilbert*

# Contents

# Acknowledgments

THIS BOOK SPRINGS from my decision to go back to school as an older and, actually, a mature adult. I didn't know it at the time but that decision to challenge my brain as a doctoral student was the beginning of a creative process that has only increased over these past ten years. Before this phase of my life, I could never have imagined writing a book. But I did, and it feels somewhat like a miracle. Of course, it isn't a miracle; it happened because of a lot of hard work on my part, which was shored up and swaddled by kind and loving people who helped, each in their own way.

At Antioch University New England, Alesia Maltz and Heidi Watts advised and led me through the daunting dissertation process. They showed me the way to completion, which I couldn't have found without them. They remain interested and encouraging as I have moved from older student to new writer. Others at Antioch shaped my thinking and process: Jean Amaral, the creative librarian; Sue Weller, the consummate administrator; and Tom Wessels, the supreme environmental sage. Barbara Vinick, my "outside" advisor and now friend, generously shared her knowledge of issues that impact older adults, and I benefited immensely from her expertise.

I made new friends at Antioch with whom I shared hard times but also universal support and encouragement. Luanne Johnson has remained a good friend and confidant. Randi Pokladnik, Twyla Dell, Amy Cabiness, and Randy Larsen are still in my life in important ways. Melissa Laser died before I could thank her personally for all that I learned from her, and I miss her intensely.

My children, who didn't think I was crazy to go back to school, have been wonderfully enthusiastic as I completed my degree, wrote and published articles, and completed this book. Endless love and thanks to my sons and daughters-in-law: Philip Eli Knapp and Vicki Ann Jackson Knapp, and Daniel Charles Knapp and Mari Hirono Knapp. Although my grandchildren—Hannah Rose Jackson Knapp, Samuel John Jackson Knapp, and Lina Sakura Hirono Knapp—were too young (or not yet born) to understand the import of getting a doctoral degree, just their presence in my life provided continuous joy and grounding.

My family members have been excited about my work, each in his or her own way: my sister Paula Ruth Gilbert and her husband Randy Gabel, my brother Arthur Gilbert and his wife Kathy Eudeikis, my sister-in-law Judy Gilbert and her husband Bill Sutherland are sources of ideas for how to get older in a planful way. My cousin Sonia Joseph and her husband Irwin Selikson are endlessly enthusiastic. My parents Anne and Louis Gilbert and my aunt Lena Bobrow have all died, but they would be very excited for me, and very likely proud of my achievement. Their lives and how they lived them in a meaningful way inspired my thinking. My aunt Sylvia Goldberg, the last member of the older generation, has been a wise and straightforward counselor. I go to her for advice when my thinking gets muddy; hers is always clear.

I have numerous friends and colleagues who always have good suggestions on my writings. They have been generous with their intimate and thoughtful discussions with me: Miriam Sack, Alan Sack, Eileen Shaevel, Annette Needle, Phyllis Paster, Lois Bienstock, Bee Franklin, Carol Greenfield, Donna Soodalter-Toman, Martha Kurz, Walter Woolf, Linda Roemer, Jeanne Stolbach, John Lowe, Harriet Tolpin, and all of the "Debs." I especially appreciate the time and thinking that Harriet Adelberg, Fredda Chauvette, Vivien Goldman, and Leon Knapp dedicated to reading and commenting on the manuscript before it went to my editor.

Staff at the Newton Department of Senior Services have read many of my articles and critiqued them prior to publication in the *Newton TAB*: Jayne Colino, Alice Bailey, Joanne Fisher, and Lynn Feinman. Jayne Colino, who is the Director of Senior Services for the city of Newton, Massachusetts, has inspired me in her dedication. She works constantly, persistently, and tenaciously to enhance the lives of all Newton seniors and their families.

My earnest thanks to Gail Spector, former editor of the *Newton TAB*, who wanted to bring senior issues into the forefront and who published each of my submitted articles. Emily Costello, the new *TAB* editor, has continued this tradition.

David O'Neil has proven to be an unbelievable mentor and friend. He taught me the ins and outs of self-publishing, was excited about the concept of my book, and continues to share his great knowledge. Without him this book would never have come together so smoothly, if at all. I thank my editor, Laurel Kayne, who challenged me in such powerful ways that I have become both a better writer and, importantly, a better reader.

Finally, I am forever grateful to my readers who tell me, over and over, that I write what they are thinking, that they made good decisions based on my words and experience, and that I should keep writing. The greatest compliment I have received was from a reader who said, "you are writing for us." Yes, I am writing for us—not about us—as I strive to represent the voices of those of us who are in the aging process and facing multitudes of decisions at this stage of our lives.

With profound gratitude, I thank you all.


Marian Leah Knapp
Welfleet, Massachusetts
October 2013

Some of life's most precious gifts can only
be acquired with age: wisdom, for example,
and mastery in hundreds of different spheres
of human experience that requires
decades of learning.

— Gene Cohen, *The Mature Mind:*
*The Positive Power of the Aging Brain*

# *Present Focus*

### Who I Am

### What I Set Out to Accomplish

# Who I Am

I AM A MEMBER of a group that is much observed and reported on by mostly well-intentioned people. I am an older adult. The literature, news, predictions, and precautions about me, and everyone else who falls into my category, is abundant. Countless perspectives are represented and reported on through all types of media. Debate abounds about my financial drain on the economy, current and future health problems, psychological and emotional challenges, impact on my family, where I might live, how I will get around, my threat as a driver, and my inevitable decline into neediness.

Certainly, there are some less dismal views about me—that I can be a contributor to society, a role model for younger people, an impetus for change, and a lifelong learner. But these commentaries seem to be outweighed by the predictions of me as a "problem adult." Within this environment and in a somewhat more upbeat vein there are also those who counsel me to follow paths and programs that will increase my chances of aging "successfully" or to stay indefinitely young. This well-meaning encouragement adds to my perplexity because the idea of being successful implies some kind of failure if I don't measure up to someone else's definition of success. Regarding eternal youth, I know the bottom-line truth because logic and experience has taught me that I will not be forever young. I will age and die just like everyone before and after me.

The writings about my aging often come from the voices of those who observe me through the lenses of their specialized viewpoint such as nutrition, medical care, or social work. Certainly, it is important that I eat right, see my doctor regularly, and try to stay connected to people. Paying attention to and learning from experts in these areas of knowledge can be helpful in dealing with specific issues. But sometimes I feel that a more holistic, inclusive view of my aging might give me insights on how to balance the multiple dimensions of my complex life. There is a certain irony that, with all these viewpoints, somehow I as a total individual am not described more clearly. In fact, as I read various perspectives, I sometimes feel I have disappeared—reduced to a collection of discrete bits and pieces to be studied, evaluated, and improved.

I believe that most of the work that is focused on me is sincere and reflects a genuine desire to make my life better in some way as I continue to age. But it is hard to know because it can be difficult to distinguish those who have genuine good intentions versus those who are only touting their own remedy for preventing me from getting older or helping me look younger by using their anti-wrinkle cream.

This leads me to wonder who I can rely on for good advice and counsel. Over the years, as I accumulated experience and knowledge, I have come to believe that some of my best insights come from me. Certainly I need the guidance of experts regarding my health, social, or financial status, but I have learned to listen to my own inner voice when it comes to making decisions about my life. I am the critical expert about me.

In addition to the tendency for others to define who I am, as an aging person, I have difficulty knowing how to categorize myself in broader societal terms. There are numerous words to describe me: elder, older adult, mature adult, senior, aged, over 65er, old-folk, golden-ager, Social Security and Medicare entitled beneficiary, retiree, even "greedy geezer." One on-line dictionary has 37 synonyms for "elder," 29 of which imply something awful such as decrepit, enfeebled, senile, or wasted.[1] According to this list of terms, I could also be seen as experienced, mature, skilled, or venerable, but the odds are stacked against me. Eighty percent of the terms associated with getting older (at least on this website) conjure up a devastatingly negative image of infirmity. If I were to assign descriptive terms to myself, I would reverse the balance and put the emphasis on mature and experienced.

Another feature of this aging categorization thing has to do with where I fall in the generational spectrum. Again, I am not quite sure where to slot myself. I'm not a World War II "Greatest Generation" member—too young. I am not a post–World War II "baby boomer"—I am too old, having missed that designation by not quite a decade. There is much talk about the Greatest Generation and much more about the baby boomers but very little about my cohort. I feel a little slighted. What about me, I wonder? Who am I? It turns out that I am a member of the "Silent" or "Forgotten" Generation along with approximately 39,000,000

---

[1] *Retrieved May 12, 2012, from thesaurus.com/browse/elder.*

others who are currently living through and dealing with getting older—just as earlier generations did in the past and upcoming generations will in the future.

Along with my thoughts on my own aging process and how others observe me, I have many reflections on the profound responsibility of being a designated caregiver, something that so many of us go through as we continue to age. I watched over numerous older loved ones, most of whom lived into their 90s. I learned firsthand both the satisfactions and the difficulties of taking care of old or disabled people. I gained insights from them and about them—the progression and richness of their lives, their achievements and frustrations, their vigor and weariness, and their memories of sadness and joy. I learned how big systems, including medicine, social services, housing, and transportation, although well intentioned, sometimes work well for older people and sometimes do not. I held the health care proxies and powers of attorney for several relatives, but was unprepared for the myriad of questions I needed to answer, either routinely or urgently, and for which I had no training. The paths to finding and gathering information, identifying issues, and making decisions were often poorly laid down, out of sync with each other, and which sometimes made no practical sense.

I learned, particularly from my mother who died at age 95, that some advanced thinking and planning was invaluable through the many years before the end of life. She was the one who decided to stop driving and move closer to family. Well in advance of old age, she had her legal and financial documents in order and made her funeral arrangements. She even tried to pay for food that might be served after her interment but the funeral parlor said they didn't do that kind of thing. She was disappointed. The situations with other relatives were not so simple because either inadequate or no thought had gone into basic "what-if," or more realistically "when," scenarios, leaving me to make very tough decisions. My care and love for them didn't suffer because of this, but the lack of clarity caused untold and unnecessary anxiety, and sadness for me.

As I watched over these beloved relatives, I realized that I could live to be as old as they and wondered, if that were the case, what I should do with the 30 or so years I may have left. My goal became to make a positive contribution for the benefit of people who were getting older and those who care for them.

# What I Set Out to Accomplish

At age 64, with these thoughts churning in my mind, I decided to go back to school to earn a doctorate and learn as much as I could about what it is like to get old. I already had some experience getting older and wanted to learn what other aging experts said. One of my hopes was that I could figure out how to make some sense of the inevitable aging process both for myself and for those who will watch over me in the future. Once I did that I could report on what I discovered and hopefully pass on some helpful clues.

I wanted to complete the degree before I reached 70—and I did. I defended and passed my doctoral dissertation, "Aging in Place in Suburbia: A Qualitative Study of Older Women," in 2008, right before my 70th birthday, and, after lots of edits, I graduated less than a year later.

In my first year of school, my advisors suggested that I study the notion of "aging in place," which initially seemed limited and uninteresting. I had accepted the 30-year-old definition that "aging in place" is "…not having to move from one's present residence in order to secure necessary support services in response to changing need."[2] The emphasis was on the home and staying there. However, the more I explored the topic in literature from diverse disciplines and compared it to my own experience as a caregiver, and an aging person, I began to realize that the simple construct of remaining at home with services didn't reflect the true complexity of the aging life and all of its facets. In the lives of the people I cared for and my own life, there were connections to many different places of which the home was only one, but I

[2] *Retrieved May 15, 2012, from seniorresource.com/ageinpl.htm*

didn't have a clear understanding of what all those places were. Even if I had been able to define those places I wouldn't have known my relationships to them. I suspected that a new view of aging in place was needed along with an understanding of the array of places in which aging happens.

In examining the demographic characteristics of older people I discovered that 50% of people age 65 and older live in a suburban community (similar to the U.S. population in general). Yet I found that very little research had been done on what it was like to grow older in a community that was built for families with young children. U.S. Census data also showed that women live longer than men and are more likely to be alone in older age. So, I framed my research to examine the experience of women who are aging in suburbia.

With these ideas in mind, I set out four goals for my study: identify the various places that comprise the total environment of aging in place; identify the factors that enabled aging in place in a suburban community; and understand the aging experience for women. The final goal was to refine and expand definitions of aging in place. My hope was that my work could be used to inform planning for the future among individuals, and agencies that serve elders and their families.

I took a qualitative approach using interviews as my data gathering method. I interviewed 20 women ages 60 to 85 who lived independently in community settings (not assisted living or nursing homes) in Newton, Massachusetts, where I live. I had no difficulty finding people to talk to and who were anxious to speak their minds. Many expressed the opinion that finally someone was actually talking to them.

I used open-ended questions about why people moved to this suburb, what life had been like for them when they first lived there, what it was for them as they got older, and what they thought their life would be in the future. To analyze my interview data, I used qualitative methods through which I developed themes. Knowing that I could not be completely objective in my analysis, I acknowledged the bias from my own history and intimate immersion in so many facets of the process of aging.

Six "places" emerged as aspects of the total environment of aging in place: home, neighborhood, local community (in this case Newton), the nearby city of Boston, the larger world, and nature. Each of these places was complex in its own way and each manifested three dimensions: physical aspects, such as location, size, and special features; a social dimension that reflected the gatherings of family and friends in that place; and an emotional dimension that included, for example, people's memories of and sense of attachment to a place. The current use of the term "aging in place" emphasizes staying in one's house and implies a reluctance to move, resistance to change, and that the only alternative is a nursing facility. In actuality, the women in my study represented a much more diverse experience that suggested that the house was not always the most significant element of their lives. In fact, many women were quite happy to be relieved of the responsibilities and potential isolation that comes with home ownership.

The factors that enabled aging in place fell into two categories. First were the characteristics of each place, which included, for example, physical suitability, safety, and available services. Second were the characteristics of the women themselves, which included resilience, economic stability (not necessarily wealth), social connections, willingness to access supports, independence, respectful relationships with children, pride in accomplishments, meaning in one's life, and a sense of belonging.

Concerning aging in suburbia, women expressed that they and their families moved to Newton to own a house, educate their children, be upwardly mobile, and participate in other aspects of what we think of as the American Dream. It emerged that these ideals were embedded in the women's worldview, as if these were the standard characteristics of normal living. They were reluctant to relinquish suburban living in spite of barriers such as stairs in the home, loss of neighborhood friendships, and lack of driving. On the whole, they seemed to have adapted themselves and their surroundings in order to stay.

Finally, the current definition of aging in place implies that staying in one's house with supports is a desired scenario, but this may not necessarily reflect the real-life experience of elders. Certainly there are those who wish to remain in a long-term, familiar environment, but there are many who are willing to find alternatives and think creatively about their aging process. My research suggests a positive way of thinking about aging would be to consider the multi-dimensional aspects of the environment in which we age and use these to make future plans that are more robust than simply finding ways to obtain support in a house. Using this notion, the challenge then became how to identify, think about, and implement forward-thinking changes. That is what this book is all about.

In framing this book, I used the basic "places" of "aging in place" that I identified through my research and compared those to my own understanding. I massaged the "places" and revised them to indicate my experience. These are outlined in the next section, and the subsequent essays explore my reflections on the places in which I am aging.

…we do not live in an abstract framework of geometric spatial relationships; we live in a world of meaning. We exist in and are surrounded by places—centers of meaning. Places are…combinations of the material and the mental and cannot be reduced to either.

— Tim Cresswell, *In Place/Out of Place: Geography, Ideology, and Transgression*

# *My Places of Aging*

# What Are My Places of Aging?

I LIVE IN A world made up of many places. I can describe myself in relationship to each of them separately but none of these pieces, in isolation, can define my total environment. Each is only a segment—part of a larger whole. But as separate concepts, they form the basis for exploring elements of my past and identifying planning pathways into the future.

## My Society and Culture

I have been shaped partially by my own personality and history, but also, to a large extent, by the greater society and culture in which I have lived. Society and culture have created categories that are supposed to define me, starting from early childhood; through teenage years; younger, middle, and older adulthood; and now older age. I have lived through most of these categories and can even describe who I was as a sweet, compliant girl; a confused teen; a searching young adult; and a responsible middle-ager. These descriptors are pretty much the accepted norm, at least for many members of my generation. The next category—that of a senior—is new territory through which I am trying to navigate. Up until fairly recently the tendency was to lump all people age 65 and older into one group, implying that we were somehow similar. Now it is more common to hear about "younger," "middle," "old," and "old old" seniors. Nevertheless, in daily life I find that misperceptions and stereotypes about me abound. I am slowly learning what they are and how I am perceived. My challenge is to acknowledge society's view, decide what to accept and what to question, and how to respond.

Some of the "mega-places" that I have dealt with along the way seem to fit in the category of larger culture and society since they have standards with which I must comply. The health care system, the legal system, and the financial system and their multitudinous sub-places all have had an impact on me. Many of the decisions that I have made concerning how I want to live my life have led to encounters with each of them—fortunately not too often. Even though these big-system places are not present in my daily life, it is here that bottom-line decisions occur in terms of health care, financial planning, legal issues with documents that spell out my wishes and who will carry them out on my behalf, and ultimately, the end of life. The big systems don't fit neatly into my schema, but I can't ignore them. If I did, I would be leaving out significant places that impact my life and the lives of people I love.

## My Natural World

I have come to appreciate the place of nature much later in my life. As a child I had little exposure to the natural world except what I could see in my city back yard and in the few family vacations at a beach or in the mountains of New Hampshire. In my teens I would sometimes wander tentatively in Roger Williams Park, but never really explored what was going on there beyond the zoo and its main attraction, Alice the Elephant. There was one tree that drew me into the park. It was close to the entrance and it was easily climbable. With a few short scrambles I could reach where the main branch split in two, forming a little V that was big enough to embrace me comfortably. I never stayed long, feeling somewhat fearful of being out there in the grass and trees all by myself. But I do recall a calming sensation of separateness and containment, along with a sense of timid independence—even a little romanticism. I remember the breezes, the sun shining down, and the fact that I never stayed for long, being worried that something scary would happen to me out there in nature.

## My Community and Neighborhood

I try to be careful when I use the word "community" because on any given day my own definition may change. My whole world, as I experience it, includes many different communities. There is the community of the city where I live and all of the resources and amenities it provides. There is a material aspect to my city—its streets, buildings, businesses, and local government. I go to meetings in city buildings, visit my local post office, and walk in nearby conservation land. This is where I live, physically. I am part of communities within and outside of my city that are comprised of congregates of people with similar interests in business, social causes, or spiritual matters. I am part of communities of old friends and colleagues, the members of which are scattered around the country. My neighborhood is a little different from how I see my other communities. It is much more definable, with a limited geographic area which I can walk around in an hour or less, and it includes my immediate neighbors. But the same distinctions of physical and "virtual" communities apply here. I am only somewhat connected to the whole of it, since I mainly know the people whose houses I can see from my windows. In these houses there are families with young children, teens on their way to or in college, single adults, and a few aging-in-placers like me. I am not much a part of their regular lives but connect in mostly casual ways, often to discuss a particular issue that affects our small enclave. It is a struggle to determine how I fit into my own multi-generational neighborhood.

## My House

Ah, my house—so much talk about my house and how important it is (or is assumed to be) in my life. It is certainly a place that surrounds me with familiarity. I feel safe here, and it suits my physical and practical needs. I have worked to make my house welcoming, both in its concrete characteristics and by offering it as a place where people can gather for celebratory events with family and close friends. It is also where one or two friends arrive to spend some peaceful time with me in soft conversation. My attachment to the social aspects of my house is greater than to the physical aspects because the real importance of my house lies in its value as a backdrop for memories involving people who are important to me. I have come to realize that no matter where I live and for however long, I can replicate this sociability to a great extent in a different space, albeit one with not as long a history with me in it. I would still be the gatherer of people, and I believe it is possible to generate new memories in a new house-place. Still, I wonder about my house, whether I should find someplace else to live or just stay where I am. I am attempting to understand the magnetism that holds me here and unpack the mysteries that make it hard to leave. It is a dilemma still unresolved but I am working on it.

## My Family and Friends

I clearly have an important place within the organic assembly of family and friends. Segments of this group are fluid as some people leave either because of special circumstances (such as moving away) or because they die. Others come into the circle as I identify relatives I never knew I had or gather in new friends as a result of common interests, experiences, and sometimes just serendipity. I see this assemblage as falling into three general categories: those from the earlier generations—my parents, aunts and uncles; my contemporaries—siblings, cousins, long-time friends; and the generations after me and beyond—my children and grandchildren. With one exception, all of the previous generation has died, most of them at advanced age. I watched over many of them at the ends of their lives. I tried to find and supply what they needed, to learn from their experiences and memories, and to gather my own impressions of their aging. They gave me profound perspective on what it is like to get through maturity, frailty, and death. My contemporaries are mostly still with me, and my place with them varies depending on where they live, the extent of our ongoing mutual interests, and the long memories we have together. My newer friends are of many different ages and have entered into my life at different times through work, school, or the community. My place with them is somewhat less burdened than some of my other relationships because we began our friendships without uncomfortable or unspoken historical baggage. I have a different place within the context of my children and grandchildren. So far, I have (fortunately) not had to depend on them for very much. Mainly I am a helper, a filler-inner—basically a very good parent and grandparent who tries to support them as they establish their lives and careers. There will be a time when my place in my children/grandchildren configuration will change. I will likely become more dependent on them, with a gradual shift from provider to "providee." I expect this shift will be extremely difficult to accept, both for them and for me. I must work on my part of it.

## My Mind and Body

The mechanism that pulls all of this together is me—the inner place of my mind and the body that holds it. Of all of my places this is the one I take with me wherever I go. I know it intimately but there are always surprises and new insights. I continue to investigate and explore it. My mind with its sheltering body interacts with all of my other places, each of which influences me in different ways. And, from time to time, I influence them. I understand the importance of keeping my body and mind in shape, but most importantly, I use them to redesign and recreate my life. I adjust my body to new constraints, and I use my mind to open up new ways of thinking about my progress through aging. Although all of my other places of aging carry rich and powerful connotations, the most powerful place is simply me. I will try to use my body to its fullest capacity and tap my mind's ability to gain knowledge, benefit from experience, make decisions, and trust my own competence.

## Conclusion

These are my places of aging. They are complex and, over time, they rise and wane in importance depending on the demands of circumstance. This means that there have been times when I had to choose where to put my energies. When I was taking care of family members, for example, I had to step back from community and neighborhood involvement. Sometimes, however, focusing on one particular place enhanced my involvement in another. Expanding my mind in school involved me in the natural world and introduced me to new friends.

These places are not discrete, disconnected categories. They merge along broad, overlapping borders. But, I have found them to be a convenient frame within which to contemplate my life. When I get stuck making a decision about what to do next I can use these places as a checklist to help me determine where and how to enrich my life.

My places may be different from yours, and you can set out to discover your own. Whether you use my categories or your individual ones, finding a context for thinking and planning during the aging years can mitigate some uncertainty about the future. Of course, we can't predict what will happen tomorrow, but most likely tomorrow will be similar to today. Thinking about ways to plan can make tomorrow different in a positive, thoughtful, and empowered way.

The temptation is to stay inside; to subside into the kind of recluse whom neighbourhood children regard with derision and a little awe; to let the hedges and weeds grow up, to allow the doors to rust shut, to lie on my bed in some gown-shaped garment and let my hair lengthen and spread out over the pillow and my fingernails to sprout into claws, while candle wax drips onto the carpet. But long ago I made a choice between classicism and romanticism. I prefer to be upright and contained—an urn in daylight.

— Margaret Atwood, *The Blind Assassin*

# *My Place in Society and Culture*

# The Silent Generation

ALMOST EVERY DAY as I read the newspaper, watch television, listen to the radio, or look through AARP publications there is talk about the Baby-Boom Generation. And from time to time I see media coverage about other generational groups like the Greatest Generation, who fought in World War II, and Generations X and Y, who came after the Boomers. But nothing about my age group.

I belong to a cohort of people who were born before and during the Second World War, roughly between 1925 and 1944. I am too old to be a "Boomer" and not old enough to be a "Greatest." Recently I began to wonder if my group had an identifier. A brief web search revealed that I belong to the Silent, or Forgotten Generation. I had lived for many years not knowing my assigned title, which was just as well. I felt a little down after discovering that my group had such a dull label, but was pleased that I had avoided that nondescript designation until now.

We Silents number about 39 million. We are viewed as an honorable group that keeps its collective nose to the grindstone and is cautious, uninspired, politically conservative, and not very vocal. As I look at myself, I do tend to embody some of these characteristics, such as hard-working and careful. But I don't fit the political profile, and I try to be enthusiastic or inspiring in my daily dealings, primarily through writing, which makes me visible and a bit noisy.

I discovered writing somewhat later in life, when I was around 65, during my doctoral studies. My dissertation research, which was on aging in place in suburbia, required that I read material from multiple disciplines on what happens to us as we get older (no matter what generational group we belong to). I found an overwhelming quantity of literature on waning bodies, minds, relationships, finances, and societal roles.

Over the years of reading I began to realize that almost everything that was written about me and my peers was from the viewpoint of doctors, social workers, physical therapists, housing specialists, psychologists, financial analysts, and many others who work with seniors. These professionals provided both encouraging and discouraging perspectives as they first acknowledged various vulnerabilities and then proposed moderating strategies. There were also heartening insights on the benefits of older age, such as the fact that mature brains integrate information more effectively than unripe ones. Also, surveys have shown that older adults are generally happier than younger people because elders have accepted what they can and cannot accomplish and are content as they move ahead.

This was all relevant and important knowledge to have. But, at some point during my studies, I had an epiphany: It struck me with stunning clarity that there was surprisingly little written by the people who were actually getting old. Where were our voices in these conversations—the authentic viewpoints of aging individuals? It was with this recognition that I began to write about me—not to self-promote, but to use myself as an example of an aging person who thinks and talks about the issues we face.

With this in mind, shortly after I finished my degree I submitted an article about the meaning of "aging in place" to my local newspaper. It was accepted. A few weeks later I submitted another article, and it too was accepted. That was not quite three years ago. I have currently published more than 30 articles about my personal experience with aging. It is wonderful that the newspaper continues to print my observations, and the responses I get from readers inspire me to continue writing.

This is what people say to me: "You are writing what I'm thinking." "I am dealing with the same issues you are talking about." "I could have written the very same article because I am going through it with my mother." Some have even said that they have made decisions based on something I said, such as clearing out old files after reading my article, "What to Do with My Stuff." I have friends all over the country who live in communities similar to mine, and I send them my articles. They pass them on to their families and friends, and I hear back the same comments as in my town.

These responses are enormously gratifying, partly because they tell me that people (perhaps of many ages) are reading my column. But much more importantly, I feel as if I am giving voice to and validating the issues and concerns that so many of us confront. However, while the issues and concerns may be common, the reach of my voice is small, and I don't hear other seniors rising up in a chorus of their own. I listen, but we seem to be largely silent—especially the Silents.

There are a number of websites and blogs geared towards older adults, and they can be helpful around specific issues. A few include comments from members of older generations, but again, much of the content is written by professional writers and practitioners about us. What I would really like to see is more commentary by us in these various forums, or perhaps we can even create new platforms for discourse. We agers are the most credible experts on our own lives, and we have a lot to share with those coming up behind us. In speaking out, we can begin to raise awareness about the fact that we elders are alive and thinking, that we have useful knowledge and insights, and that we are not alone in our lives and thoughts. Also, sharing our knowledge with those who will face similar issues in the future may add valuable perspective to their own decision making.

I think that Silents are wonderfully positioned to do this. We can choose not to be so silent. Right now I feel as if I am an outlier because I haven't been able to find anyone else like me willing to put it all out there. Also, opportunities for making an older voice heard are not easy to come by. My generation isn't readily being handed a microphone. But maybe my local effort is a promising start.

What about other Silents? What if there were more of us sharing our thoughts and experiences about the complex dimensions of our lives? What if every local or even national newspaper had an aged writer who addressed substantive age-related issues from an elder point of view? Many newspapers and local media cover what is happening at their senior centers and Councils on Aging, which is very important. But this is not what I am talking about. I am pushing the idea that we Silents have the power to be a positive force for raising consciousness and promoting positive actions on behalf of all seniors—no matter what generation we belong to. By remaining silent we help to foster negative stereotypes about elders because we are not showing who we are as whole persons. I don't want other voices to define who I am.

I am hopeful that there are many out there who think as I do. We who have the most experience have lots to say. We have an opportunity, and I want to grab it. I have started small and will continue to write in my local sphere. But we all need to figure out what we can do together to create a broad sweep of understanding. Silence is never a good way to make positive, forward-thinking change.

# Good Enough Aging

Lately I have been reading up on "successful aging" to understand better what people mean when they use the term. I thought it would be helpful to figure out what significance it may have for me and to see whether I am living up to whatever the goals and standards of successful aging should be. I must admit that the term strikes me as a little odd. Success for me is achieving a goal that is personally meaningful, has a tangible outcome, and for which I worked hard. How does this notion of success apply to getting older?

John W. Rowe and Robert L. Kahn in their oft-cited book, *Successful Aging,* say that successful aging means "…aging well…" and that the "…three main components of successful aging [are] avoiding disease and disability, maintaining mental and physical function, and continuing engagement in life" (p. 68). They go on to explore the differences between younger and older people on these dimensions, noting that older people are often at higher risk in all of them. So, successful aging seems to mean a lot of what I know already—the things that will help me move into the future in the best way possible.

I recognize that keeping my brain active, exercising my body, eating sensibly, being involved in my community, and staying connected to family and friends will help me be "successful." But, fundamentally, I must be the one to define what successful aging is for me and how high or low to set my targets. At this point in my life (actually any point), I will not strive for great athletic prowess—I can set this threshold fairly low. Try to walk 3-4 times a week, maybe. I eat pretty sensibly but my poundage has crept up over the years. Will I ever get back to my high school graduation weight? Probably not. Should I try to lose a few pounds so that I don't feel guilty every time I get on the scale? Yes—we'll see.

Being connected to my community is pretty important because I know the value of learning about and being involved in the place where I live. It's great to walk down the street being able to say "hi!" to an increasing number of people. My world is getting bigger, not shrinking. I set this target modestly high. Keeping my brain active—this is way up there on the list. Not being able to learn, think, write, and be creative would present a real problem for me emotionally and psychologically. I have set this as an important priority and I work at it almost every day.

The biggest one is staying connected to family and friends, both old and new. These important relationships preserve long-time memories and build new ones. Old memories encourage me to learn from the past, while giving me constant fuel for moving ahead. My family and friendships cushion and buoy my ongoing life.

As I look at the things that are important to me, the notion of aging "well" seems more apt than aging "successfully." Success feels rigid. "Well" feels less intimidating but still implies a standard that I may, or may not, be able to achieve.

This brings me to the idea of "good enough aging." I didn't invent this term. It comes from my sister-in-law, who has thought a lot about the importance of identifying and accepting what is "good enough." Here are some simple examples. When she did work on her kitchen the new counters weren't perfect, but they served their purpose and she decided they were good enough—saving herself the hassle and expense of redoing them for little gain. Similarly, when she makes a meal for a large gathering she realizes that what she serves may not fully satisfy every guest, but she tries hard to make a meal that most people will like. Rather than strive for unattainable perfection, with its attendant stress, she aims for good enough and can enjoy a special evening with a sense of calm.

These little stories don't reflect the complex nature of getting older, but they help me put my life in a new context. Within this "good enough aging" construct I feel at peace with what I have accomplished—raising kids, caring for elders, spending time with grandkids, being involved with communities and friends, keeping my body in reasonable shape, learning and growing my mind, and looking forward to writing my next article. I expect I won't be "successful" according to some extreme, perhaps mean-ingless, goals (like living to be 100), but I do anticipate that my "good enough" attitude will keep me moving along from one day to the next without getting bogged down in the unattainable.

This is a very freeing concept. I don't have to push myself to do things I don't want to do. I can emphasize and pay attention to what is most important according to my own values. I don't have to compare myself to someone else's potentially unrealistic (or un-important) criteria, but set my standards consistent with what is doable and has meaning for me—that's good enough.

# Elders Are Not Like Children

A number of years ago, my aunt Celia participated in an activity that brought older people (she was in her late 80s) and young children together. The goal was to create a video that showed them having fun together. I remember asking her what she thought about the project. She shrugged her shoulders, acted a little uncomfortable, and said something like, "I really don't know." I didn't have the foresight to ask her what she meant, but I do remember that I felt a lot of discomfort after watching the completed video. Unfortunately, I can't ask Celia how she felt about the experience because she has died, as have most of the members of that older generation.

Celia, who was 93 at her death, was a very independent, positive-thinking person who took care of herself, often on her own, for a good deal of her life. She had a lot of experience, knowledge, and maturity. What struck me about the video project was that the producers seemed to have no idea about who Celia or any of the other older people in the production were as individuals. The focus was on childlike games and gimmicks—perfectly appropriate for kids, but not really for Celia.

I don't quite remember what the film's message was, but I recall people jumping out of hidden places, making funny faces and noises, and wearing silly costumes. To me, the younger/middle-age director seemed to convey the notion that older people had the same idea of fun as kids. I was unsettled. I couldn't figure out what the director was thinking or what assumptions he was making about older people. Did he believe that he could equate mature older people's ideas of having a good time with those of immature children who had very little life experience? I have no doubt that he was trying to do something good by bringing seniors and children together, but the message seemed to enforce stereotypes that equate old age with childlike behavior.

There are studies on the benefits of older and younger people working together, but this research usually involves some meaningful activity—like the exchange of ideas, storytelling, or art. This video, which was done ten years ago, showed nothing but childishness, reinforcing the notion that being old is being infantile. I'll never know what impact or exposure this tiny media experiment had on the participants or those who viewed it, but I'm sure it was small. Times are different now. Media has exploded and the messages we see are viewed by millions of people every day.

One recent program that specifically set out to give exposure to older people is *Off Their Rockers* with Betty White. The theme of the show is to show older people deceiving innocent bystanders by doing outrageous things. I watched only a small number of episodes before having that same feeling that elders were being stereotyped and, perhaps, degraded by having them do childish things. Only this time they were depicted as crass connivers rather than little kids. Seniors were shown as tricksters who were obsessed with sex ("dirty old men"), getting out of paying the bill ("greedy geezers"), trapping people in embarrassing and confusing situations ("manipulators"), crashing into objects while in a wheelchair ("incompetent"), or asking ridiculous questions ("senile"). In contrast, most of the targets of the tricks were young people who seemed innocent, accepting, concerned, and wanting to help out. That was nice to see and diminished some of my own stereotypical notions of young people as self-absorbed and callous.

The message that a 90-year-old like Betty White can still be creative and fun-loving is great because, in reality, that is what many old people are. But it is unfortunate that the subject matter of her program denigrated positive perceptions of aging by perpetuating nasty stereotypes about being old.

Stereotypes are so embedded in our psyches that we often don't know they are there, and it takes a lot of effort to bring them out and confront them. I wonder how many people watch *Off Their Rockers* and see just a funny sitcom. Of course there is no doubt that the intent of both *Off Their Rockers* and Celia's video is to make people laugh by using a goofball approach in which the subjects are portrayed as silly or bumbling. I am not a fan of this genre in general, but it goes from annoying to offensive for me when it involves older people. Instead of a comedic style, all I see is an unpleasant, damaging, and I think prevalent stereotype. I am not dumb or bungling, and neither are the elders I know now or have ever known. But it seems that our competence is easy for people to overlook. And it's even easier to get a laugh by portraying us as childish, foolish, and mindless.

To help confront this stereotype, I have embarked on a continuing campaign. On a personal level, in everyday conversations, I simply acknowledge that I'm a senior, and when I talk, I try to say thoughtful things even when it is small talk. I try to show that I think about important ideas in reasonable ways. In my public life, I write about making plans and decisions, and then acting on them decisively but not rashly. I also describe my involvement in the civic and political workings of my community as an advocate for older people and those who are involved in their lives.

I could just talk about the problem, but that is not enough. I am working to personify another image—that of a positive, contributing, mature, and thoughtful person. This is nothing new. We older people have always been this way. It's just that we haven't established a good way to show who we are. I'm working hard to change that, at least for myself.

# Older and Visible

I am probably similar to many women who are getting older. Every morning I look in the mirror and notice the wrinkles in my cheeks and the slightly puffy pouches under my eyes. I wonder if other people notice. "My glasses will cover the baggy eyes and a little make-up will give some smoothness and color to my skin," I mull and then turn away, dismissing those thoughts for the rest of the day. Usually, I try not to think too much about the annoying aspects of my own aging except in these brief moments in front of the mirror or when minor episodes of arthritis in my thumbs make it hard to open a jar. Friends who are my age have similar worries, and some have much more serious problems. I consider myself lucky. But what is lurking behind my brief explorations of my aging face?

According to commonly accepted concepts of what being "older" is, I'm not getting older...I am already there. True, I might be categorized as "younger" old (compared to "middle," "older," or "oldest" old), but I am still slotted into the "older" designation by the agencies and organizations that determine such things. I reached the standard age of retirement more than eight years ago when I turned 65, and I'm eligible for Social Security. My membership in AARP, which began at age 50, offers me information, advocacy, and perks. They lobby with federal and local agencies to sustain or increase my benefits. I appreciate what AARP does, but I know people who shun membership; some won't even tell cinema box-office personnel that they are a senior because they'd rather give up their discount than admit that they are older.

I understand how they feel. I struggle with the tension between accepting the facts and signs of aging, and wanting to be seen as young, vibrant, and competent. Simply put, I want to be seen as a whole, multi-dimensional person who isn't dismissed—or perhaps worse, overlooked entirely—because she looks older. I think my mirror investigations are simply to check how much I may have aged overnight, but also to make sure I am still visible, at least to myself.

AARP can tell me about famous people like Robert Redford (75) and Bruce Springsteen (62) who are seniors, and I can hold them up as good examples of what it means to age productively. But it is easy for them to stay visible. They have star status and a powerful media that is happy to cover their comings and goings. But I am not a famous person. I'm just me, someone who is fearful of a time when I might become invisible.

Several years ago I made a presentation to residents at an assisted living facility. I talked about aging and how ageism creeps insidiously into our lives. One woman raised her hand and said that when she went out to lunch one day, the server turned to her daughter and asked, "What does she want to eat?" The woman told me, "I felt invisible." I don't really know why the restaurant employee ignored this hoary-headed patron, but I will make the assumption that there were no bad intentions. My guess is that the waitress was just reflecting common and deeply embedded cultural perceptions that silver hair and furrowed skin somehow means that there is little mental functioning behind the obviously aged face.

There is a strong push/pull tension between accepting the reality of aging and the pressure—and often desire—to appear young, and I feel it. On the one hand, I am not afraid of saying I am older; I kind of like it. I'm proud of what I have accomplished so far and excited about planning for my future. But, in contradiction to my readiness to tell people my age, I wait for the person who is selling the movie ticket to act surprised when I ask for the discount. I don't want anyone to perceive me as old. When strangers offer to help me, I usually reject it. They are being courteous and thoughtful, but they too may be caught in a different kind of dilemma, also related to my age. "Hmm, if I ask her if she needs help will I insult her? If I don't offer to help her will she think I am callous and rude?" The stranger and I have something in common. We share a lack of tradition and, therefore, a quandary. We don't know how to interact with each other in a mutually recognized way.

Our culture has not provided us with meaningful approaches for acknowledging and accepting aging in a way that honors the process. We seem not to know how to value and respect the wisdom that has often accrued by this stage of life, and we are not confident enough to challenge older people in positive ways. This can all perpetuate the potential for invisibility because it is simpler to ignore the problem—and the person—than figure out what to do. It is much easier to maintain the status quo.

So, what is the appropriate and socially acceptable response, from me and from others who see me? For those whom I may meet on the subway or in a restaurant, I caution you not to judge my competence. Without talking to me and getting to know me, you will have no idea who I really am, how complicated and reflective my life is, and how I can form and express opinions, and make decisions—including what to order for lunch. For myself, I must write about these issues, be active in my community, and engage people in good conversation. This is what I need to do to continue being visible. Otherwise I risk joining the ranks of so many older people who fade, shrink, and disappear in the eyes of strangers. Or, one day I could look in the mirror and not notice my image there—worse, I could stop looking altogether—having become invisible even to myself.

Allowing invisibility to creep up on me would be a personal calamity. Every day, week, and, yes, every moment, for as long as I have the mental power, I must sustain my self-awareness. Then I must show anyone I meet that I have a working mind and a vital spirit, and I am still absolutely, and clearly, visible.

# What Is It About the Senior Center?

The city where I live has a population of about 84,000, with about 19,000 people (close to 22%) age 60 and over. We have a Department of Senior Services, which includes a Senior Center where older people come to be involved in many different ways. There is also a Council on Aging, which acts as an advisory group to the Department. I have written for the local newspaper about my involvement with the Council. As I have been a member and chairperson of this group for several years and know how it works, the writing was an easy task for me.

To let readers know about the Senior Center, I decided to write about the wonderful things that happen there. However, I started to run into trouble when I began to frame the essay. As soon as I started writing, I felt uneasy and realized I was in a quandary. I sometimes volunteer at Senior Center programs, run focus groups with a colleague, and have meetings there often. But in reality, I don't participate. How could I talk about the Senior Center when mainly what I know is from reading the newsletter, what I hear at Council meetings, and listening to people who work or take advantage of programs there? I also wondered, more significantly, why don't I participate?

When I write, my mode is to talk about things I know. It is only from this perspective of intimate personal experience and knowledge that I can write with credibility. I can't be a dispassionate reporter on someone else's experiences. If I tried to write in this way, I know my own feelings would sneak in, and that doesn't feel honest. I try to write what I've experienced. This gives me confidence in my words and is what fuels my inspiration.

My first concern was about crafting an article that contradicted my objective of being an honest writer; I just didn't feel I knew enough about the Senior Center to write about it from my own vantage point. The second concern emerged as I reflected further and realized my own buried ageist views, which I then had to confront. I could say that I don't go to the Senior Center because for much of what is offered there I go elsewhere. I have friends and family with whom I go to the movies, take day trips, or eat and talk. So, I don't need the Senior Center for those things.

But deep down (and I acknowledge this with shame) I don't join in because I think that the people who go there are not really like me. They are old and getting older, and I don't want to associate with "them"—even though I have been a senior for a while now. I see them as others, outside me, different, and with stereotypical characteristics that don't mirror how I think about myself. With all that I write about aging, talking about issues that we seniors worry about, and presenting it in a meaningful way, this felt quite insincere. I could rationalize my discomfort by saying I didn't need the Senior Center, but that didn't calm my deep struggle with my conscience.

OK, I thought, perhaps if I got some more information I would be convinced to take advantage of their programs or services. Maybe logic and objectivity would dispel my own bias. The Center's calendar gave me more detail about what participants did. They exercised their bodies in eight different classes, learned one of five languages, received information from health and insurance experts, gained computer skills, played or listened to classical or swing music, joined in pool or bridge, talked to local officials, got advice from social workers, saw movies, painted, potted plants or wrote essays, went to museums or theaters, arranged for transportation, obtained names of people who could do minor household repairs, or simply came to find other people to talk to. It appeared as a place dedicated to enhancing community and personal life, in a vibrant, learning, health-promoting environment.

Having looked at the Senior Center with some objectivity, I asked myself again, why don't I participate? There it was once more—the ugly specter of my own ageism. Where did this come from? Perhaps I was fearful that once I put myself among other seniors I would be perceived as elderly by people of all ages who are as ageist as I am. Maybe by associating too much with other older people I would take on some characteristics that I have judged to be unattractive, like frail and needy. This is a pretty difficult thing to admit but, unfortunately, it felt real.

What to do? The first was to confront myself. I knew this wouldn't be easy. It seemed daunting to face up to the harsh realities of my own prejudices. The second was to do something practical to get more connected with the Center, such as exercise. I do walk—but not enough. I have known this for many years. "OK, go try aerobics at the Senior Center," I told myself. I can fit it into my schedule, and it would benefit my body and improve my life because I know I feel better when I am physically active. I was enthusiastic about the idea.

The truth is that I wrote the first draft of this article more than a year ago and I have still not exercised at the Senior Center. I guess I haven't accepted the fact that I am part of the flow into the oldest of the old. I must recognize this, somehow, but really don't know how. My societal and personal prejudices are still a very, very powerful force within me.

# Advocating for Myself in the Health Care System

I have an intermittent relationship with the health care system, which I envision as a gigantic conglomeration made up of thousands of parts. I usually enter into it through a single individual—my primary care physician. She sends me for tests or procedures, each of which has its own multi-tiered complexity. I would like to believe that each of the health care entities with which I interact knows what the other is doing and that they communicate. But I know that this isn't true.

Mostly I've had pretty good luck with health care, but I have had a few unpleasant events that make me increasingly watchful and aware of my crucial role as an advocate for myself. The most unpleasant incident, one with long-term (but not serious) consequences, was having a blepharoplasty—an awful name for simple eyelid surgery. Having to have this procedure was embarrassing. I kept telling people it was not because I wanted to look younger but because my eyelids had drooped so much that I was beginning to have trouble with peripheral vision. It had gotten so bad that it threatened my ability to pass the Motor Vehicle Department's vision test. Even my health insurance covered it, which helped convince me that it wasn't just for vanity.

In the pre-op period I was informed about the process and the risks and received instructions for what to do afterwards. I was asked if I had any allergies. "Yes," I said. "Neosporin ointment." This seemingly innocuous allergy had been in my electronic medical record for decades, so nothing new. Years ago I had a miserable reaction when I used Neosporin after ear-piercing. My lobes got swollen, fiery red, and intensely itchy. To be certain that Neosporin was the culprit, I did a test on my arm and the same thing happened. So I always made sure that this was in my record, and I mentioned it each time I saw a provider. I was happy that it wasn't a serious thing.

On the day of the surgery, I told the prep-nurse and she recorded it. My mistake was that I did not remind the surgeon, assuming that she had read the notes and my medical record. The surgery went well, and when I was discharged I received a tiny tube (about 1/2 inch long) with teeny writing on it. I got instructions to use the ointment several times a day. Even if my eyes had been in perfect condition, I would have had trouble reading the miniscule list of ingredients, but with post-surgically swollen eyelids, there was no way I could decipher the word "Neosporin."

A rash on earlobes or arms was no big deal, but on tender, stitched-up eyelid incisions it was a nightmare. My eyelids became inflamed, bubbly with little sores, and intolerably itchy. It was hard to sleep. For weeks I held ice-packs on my eyes, and when I went back several times to the doctor I was told I had "sensitive skin," insinuating that the cause was my body's inadequacy.

After stopping the ointment, my eyes gradually got better but never completely. Still, after almost two years, my eyelids get puffy. Itchy bumps are embedded under the skin, and my eyes feel sore at times. I expect I will have this for the rest of my life.

I can't complain too much about this episode. In the spectrum of all of the things that could go wrong, this was on the low end. Yet something did go wrong, and responsibility lies both with the surgeon and with me. She should have known what was in my chart and noticed that the medication would be problematic. I should have reminded her as many times as necessary to make sure that she was aware. I needed to be a far better advocate for me.

Knowing the pressures that health care providers are under and the mountains of information they have to absorb, I realize that it is my job to assume a greater role in my health-related care. This means that I have to become informed, learn the impact of procedures and medications, be willing to tell my provider what I know, and doggedly challenge any assumptions that don't fit with my own understanding. It may be hard to do. Certainly health care providers have a lot more technical knowledge than I do. But I am an expert on me, and I must trust my own insights. I need to get better at being stubborn and maybe a little pushy. My safety and well-being depend on it, and I can't rely on anyone else to do it for me.

I discovered my connection to the
land through the woods of my childhood.
Now when I wander through the forests
and fields that surround my home,
I am not just a tourist passing through,
but a part of the landscape—
a partner in its dialogue.

— Tom Wessels, *Reading the Forested Landscape:*
*A Natural History of New England*

# *My Place in the Natural World*

### The Benefits of Spending Time in Nature

### Storms, Pictures, and Memories

### Small-Scale Nature

### Pink Lady's Slipper

# The Benefits of Spending Time in Nature

I GREW UP IN a city triple-decker. In the back of the house there was a plantless, dusty yard that turned to mud in the rain. Nothing blossomed there. The only tree I remember from my early childhood was the one that grew in the drab, crumbling playground next to our driveway. Around this tree was one of those circular wooden benches where young mothers sat and watched their children play in the sandboxes and talked about things I never heard or cared about. My father loved the outdoors and nature, and on occasional trips to New Hampshire he would try to impart his passion for the glory of the White Mountains to my siblings and me. I don't know how my brother and sister reacted, but much of his intense feeling was lost on me. I didn't quite get it. As I came into my teen and young adult years I had only a bit more exposure to the out-of-doors, but when I moved to the suburbs as a young mother with small children I wanted my kids to understand and appreciate a part of living with which I had had limited involvement. I had to read up on natural things before going out for walks with them in the neighborhood. I learned what "Roxbury puddingstone" was and could explain how it was formed more than 500 million years ago from small pebbles and ancient lava flows, and that it was the bedrock for much of eastern New England. The little stream in back of the elementary school was a place to find tadpoles and where I could tell my children how pollywogs became frogs.

Over the many years since then, I have learned about a little more than rocks and frogs, and have gained immense respect for the spectacle of the natural world. This has come about because I have purposely prodded myself to look and listen with intent. Finally, after all these years, I am beginning to understand my dad's veneration of nature's beauty. I have learned to let nature embrace me in a way that is different from the warmth of my house. Now when I walk in the woods I notice the dazzling patterns of light on the ground and how they change when the wind blows through branches. I have become enamored of the velvety look of mosses when they are wet and the astonishing variety of lichens on dead tree limbs. Mostly, though, I cherish the peace I feel when I am in an outdoor space where there is quiet all around me except for the swish of dry leaves in the fall and the jumbled sounds of birds whose names I still don't know. When I go on walks with my young grandson in the little wooded area near my house, I find that I talk very softly—almost in a whisper. He does the same thing. He, unlike me at his age, gets it. Recently when we talked about the things we liked in the woods, he showed me a fallen tree and how the rotted end swirled inward and disappeared into darkness that our eyes couldn't penetrate.

I have found that these precious, peaceful moments in nature expanded the joy I felt when I or someone close to me achieved an important goal, or when I heard the terrific news each time I was to become a grandmother. Nature soothes me and feeds my spirit when there are tough decisions to make and losses to embrace. Several springs ago when my vibrant, 40-year-old friend—an environmental scholar and activist—died suddenly, I found sad solace imagining her spirit in simple, intense displays of nature.

Where I live there is a conservators group that works to sustain the natural parts of developed and undeveloped land. I talked to its president. She understands these life issues of sadness and joy and talked about the positive, reflective value in being outdoors. "There is spiritual nourishment to be found in nature," she says. "Through it you can develop a fuller appreciation of life in all its forms—it is all there in front of you. We tend to think of ourselves as separate from the natural world but we are not; we are part of it."

She is right. I have found that being in the natural world has helped me put things in perspective, as long as I take the time to linger in places that are different from my everyday haunts. "The natural world is so much slower than our sometimes frenetic, anxious lives," she continued. "It is perfect for reflection, especially for people as they get older. There is so much to experience. Sit quietly on a bench by the river for an hour and watch the vibrant world around you. This ever-changing scene of birds, insects, mammals, and plants is something to learn from and wonder about." Simply noticing, I have found, helps me put my life in a larger context and offers a different perspective on my own ever-changing life-stage.

Although I appreciate the benefits of nature more and more, I often need a gentle push to get out of doors. I don't have to go very far to find places to walk, sit, and think. Parks and conservation areas are all around me. There are many small or large choices—near rivers, lakes, woods, or meadows. Some can be challenging, with sharp inclines and complicated pathways; others are flat and easy to walk, with benches for sitting; and some are, amazingly, hidden from busy streets and bustling neighborhoods by just a few yards of colorful trees and shrubs. I know how to find them, but I am negligent about setting this as a priority, even though I know that is where I can find peace, solace, and wonderment.

# Storms, Pictures, and Memories

I am struck by how nature can create the backdrop for stories, long-lasting memories, and sometimes meaningful lessons. Much of the time I deal with natural phenomena only when they throw themselves upon me. In 2011, for example, the incessant winter storms and vast accumulations of snow had a major impact on my comings and goings. I have pictures that make my house look as if it is about to be swallowed up by monstrous snow mounds. I made it through those months with some minor house damage and a few memories—mainly of how sick and tired I was of the snow.

Another set of winter memories comes from the blizzard of 1978, when the storm was so overwhelming that driving was prohibited for many days. Some people may have gotten to their jobs on public transportation, but mostly the streets were vacant and people were at home. It was quiet, and neighbors serenely connected with each other, having nowhere to go. My family and I were among the lucky ones who didn't lose anyone in this devastation, but 73 people died in Massachusetts, and hundreds were rescued from buried vehicles. We hunkered down and kept warm and safe. Pictures show my kids, who were nine and thirteen at the time, dwarfed by snow piles.

Some of my most powerful recollections about storms come from September of 1938 when the "hurricane of the century" hit New England. I was only seven weeks old, so I don't have any of my own memories, but the events and the power of that day were recounted again and again by my parents. My mom was at home alone with my 2-year-old brother and me in Providence. My dad had gone to Worcester on business earlier that day or maybe the day before. They must have known a storm was coming, but the predictions didn't suggest that it would hit where it did. Without warning, the hurricane barreled into Rhode Island and pushed the Providence River into downtown, flooding it. High-water markers still exist as evidence of what happened in this storm of all storms. Old films and photos from coastal areas show people on beaches or porches watching nature show itself and then, seconds later, those figures were gone—washed away. My father managed to get home and we all ended up safe, but the power of the hurricane remained in my memory through the stories that I was raised with.

About 64 years later, in 2002, I took a course on the ecology of southern New Hampshire. One day our instructor, Tom Wessels, took us on a field trip. It was a beautiful early spring day. I remember the way the fragmented light sprinkled across the forest floor, and how the shadows increased as we walked farther into the woods. We were gently instructed to stop, to be quiet, and to observe. I remember no sound—although that was probably not the case in this old stand of trees. "Look at the forest floor," Tom said. "What do you see?" I saw lush green moss and lichen extending as a blanket into the distance. "Look more closely." I began to see even ripples—rows of narrow, slightly-raised mounds interspersed with long hollows made soft by the green growth that covered all surfaces. "What do you think caused that pattern of rising and falling?" No one responded—more silence. "It was the 1938 hurricane," he said.

I was astonished. My hurricane stories revolved around the devastation and force of water on the shore. But there was also a story in this northern forest, up in New Hampshire, far from the sea, when the 1938 winds blew down acres and acres of trees.

They fell in the same direction, millions of them, all pointing northwestward, all obliterated by the same force of nature that destroyed life and property on the coast. I can't change my hand-me-down memories, but this revelation suddenly broadened my understanding of the vast devastation that happened that day so many years ago.

Of the students who were there that day I was the only one with memories—albeit retold memories—of that storm. I wanted to shout out, "That was the year I was born!" But I didn't, perhaps not wanting to interfere with the learning of the moment but more likely not wanting to reveal my age so blatantly.

I don't have any pictures from this forest visit, but when I conjure up that day, I first picture the dense, mottled green of the woodland carpet. The image fills me with peace and calm. But next I experience a little jolt when I have to reconsider, reinterpret, and expand the limited context of my adopted memories. I had never made much of an effort to question my understanding of the vastness and force of this natural catastrophe. It was only at that instant in the woods that I realized the immense impact on places and people for whom there were consequences and recollections so very different from my own.

I could have gone to that forest on my own and walked on the layer of mosses amid the tall, thin trees. But I would never have seen the history laid out before me; it had to be pointed out. Because of this experience, now I try to seek out opportunities to learn, listen, and watch very, very carefully. There is likely to be some important lesson embedded in my surroundings that will challenge me in some unknown but powerful way. This is how I will continue to grow into my future.

# Small-Scale Nature

I have been going to Cape Cod for more than 40 years, in particular to a little plot of land in one of the narrowest sections of this fragile peninsula. What draws me back year after year is not only family tradition but phenomena that I have absorbed endlessly through my senses—visual images, sounds, tactile sensations, smells, and unique tastes, which after so many years have become embedded in my spirit.

Mostly when I describe this part of the Cape to those who don't know it well, I talk about the ocean and how each year the Atlantic carves out vast chunks of sand dunes, sometimes causing houses to fall into the sea and beach parking lots to be destroyed and rebuilt—only farther inland. The ponds, I tell people, are kettle ponds—holes in the ground that were created when the ice sheets withdrew, leaving roundish frozen chunks forming pits that ultimately filled with water. Then there are the bayside beaches and marshes—different from the peaceful ponds, much calmer than the constant ocean turmoil, and good for young children to roam around in and squish their toes in the sandy, muddy flats. There are distinct smells here, especially at low tide when large expanses are exposed and the remnants of oysters, horseshoe crabs, and dying marsh plants give off their own special aromas as they decay in place.

There is definitely grandness to the overall landscape. But what I like most are the small happenings that I notice on simple, quiet walks down the road to Loagy Bay. Some of these events can be quite dramatic—in a small-scale way. On my route, after passing a built-up area I come to the brackish marsh that houses a multiplicity of little living things. One of the larger inhabitants is the diamondback terrapin—now on the threatened species list in Massachusetts. Twice each spring females emerge from the wetland to lay their eggs in sandy dry soil. They are very determined. With their heads and necks stretched out they march forward towards a destination that only they know. The problem is that in this particular place they have decided to cross the road—albeit a small one—to get to their egg-laying spot, putting them in harm's way. In fact, before everyone knew the plight of these creatures, running them over was sometimes a sport. Now most people know and most are kind.

I have met some of these terrapins during my walks and try to do the right thing, but it isn't easy. I have picked up several that were in the middle of the road to move them across in the direction they were headed. They didn't like it. They hissed and flailed their legs, and sometimes scratched me. I've seen others try to dig their holes in the loose sand at the road's edge where they are sure to be hit by a careless driver. Moving them was a challenge because if I tried to shift them to a safer spot they just turned around and walked back into danger. Don't they know I am trying to help them?! Other people worry about them too and construct little enclosures to prevent scavengers from eating the eggs and hatchlings.

There is another lovely aspect to this walking route—it ends up at a serene beach. Thousands, maybe even millions, of fiddler crabs live here. They are pretty small, maybe one to two inches. The striking thing about these little beings is that one claw is much bigger than the other one. They live just beneath the surface in the sand and dig holes that they scurry into when someone like me appears to threaten them. Before disappearing, though, they stand their ground for a bit and brandish their outsized claw in anger. I try very hard not to step on them or their dens. What I like best about these fiddlers is not so much their posturing but the sound they make as they retreat. If I walk slowly and carefully, and then stop to listen, I can hear the rustling, rattling sound of their flight to safety. If I stand for a minute or so, the din dies down and they come out to look around. If I take another step, the clatter starts all over again. With each step on the beach I can see fiddlers retreating in the distance like an undulating wave of movement and sound that makes it seem as if the sand itself is alive.

There are things that grow in the ground along this roadway. Beach plums are mostly dying out in this stretch, but in the past I, with my kids and grandkids, have picked enough to make a few tiny jars of incredibly intense-flavored jam—only enough to make it through a half-dozen English muffins. It takes much work to make this jam from little beach plums with big pits. There is the sorting, washing, boiling, sieving, adding water, and boiling again. Finally, after perhaps a few days we have some jam. In addition to savoring the memory of the flavor, I loved the ping sound that the beach plums made when they were tossed into the pot.

Several other plant things that I have collected here are sea pickles and wild blueberries (the taste of cultivated fruit can't compete with wild flavor). The blueberries are gone now, but there used to be enough for blueberry pancakes. There are other, more prolific blueberry-picking places, and when I was younger and more willing to brave the mosquitoes there was often enough for several blueberry betties.

Sea pickle still grows in abundance in small clumps. It is green and skinny with little bumps on it. I like to just pick it and eat it on the spot. It is crunchy and very salty. It tastes like the sea. Sometimes I bring some home to put in a salad, but enjoying it right there, outside, close by the nesting terrapins and the scurrying fiddlers, looking west across the bay is just the best. At the end of my walk I return to my little haven, pour a glass of wine—cold, crisp white is lovely, especially after the salty pickle—and I watch the large, majestic sun set through the blackness of the trees. Nature, large and particularly small, is all around me.

# Pink Lady's Slipper

When I first started going to Cape Cod I learned a lot about the things that lived and grew there, including species that were deemed to be vulnerable in some way. In fact, for a long time a wooded area across the road was closed to development while a huge debate occurred about whether some plants that lived there were endangered or threatened. I don't remember all the various plants that were discussed, but one of them was the lady's slipper. The debate must have ended at some point because many houses were eventually built. My guess is that the people who bought and lived in those houses never knew what the land looked like before they arrived, or even that there had been a lady's slipper controversy.

I hadn't thought much about this history for many years until one spring day, maybe twenty years ago, I looked out at a tree close to my house and there, sitting quietly among the decades-old fallen pine needles, was a lone, vibrantly pink lady's slipper. As far back as I could remember—perhaps another twenty years—I had never seen her before. I had learned enough from the years of disagreements about threatened local plants to know that I had to be quite cautious around this brave little flower—an orchid actually. So, whenever I went out to look at it, I treaded carefully. I looked at it from every angle and noticed how it rose out of a nest of thick, short, pointed, vibrant green leaves, and how it glowed when the sun shone through its delicate, fuchsia, skin-like pouch. It was mysterious, quite sensual, and very compelling. Every spring when I returned I would check to see if the lady's slipper had survived the winter. If I saw the green leaves poking through, I knew that all was well. My lady's slipper seemed to be a very guarded but determined individual—almost trying to hide herself within this scruffy stand of trees and the delicate, spindly groundcover. She had hidden herself well. Perhaps she felt vulnerable because she didn't have a group of likewise plants to protect her with their greater numbers and visibility. No one would ever know that she was there, except me.

Then, one year when I checked the spot for emerging leaf tips, I found ten, maybe fifteen, lady's slipper plants surrounding this one tree. Some were quite noticeable, others semi-hidden as they pushed upwards through the growth and woodland debris. It was a small area, probably only a few yards around. Over several weeks I watched as a little stand of magnificently hued lady's slippers matured and encircled the tree on all sides. It was all quite exotic and daring—all of this deep, rich color in the dull green and brown wood. As time passed and the flowers shriveled up and died, I began to think about the next year, excited about seeing this display again, but I was disappointed. In subsequent years there were either no lady's slippers or maybe one or two. That rich parade of color hasn't happened again. But I'm optimistic, and I am waiting. Each spring I look carefully around the tree, stepping softly on the spongy ground, anticipating another spectacular pageant of pink, or at least one—my "one." I have learned to be very patient.

I could try to find other places that may have lady's slippers, but I desist. Maybe I don't want to spoil my relationship with this one secreted flower and any companions that could show up. I only look at this one tiny spot, around one tree. If my lady's slipper isn't there I shove her image to the back of my mind—at least until the next season. I guess I like the mystery of not knowing if she will appear from one year to another. This uncertainty always gives me something to look forward to. It provides me with a miniscule annual mission. I just hope she doesn't wait for twenty years to show herself again.

"Community" means different things to different people. We speak of the community of nations, the community of Jamaica Plain, the gay community, the IBM community, the Catholic community, the Yale community, the African American community, the 'virtual' community of cyberspace, and so on. Each of us derives some sense of belonging from among the various communities to which we might, in principle, belong.

— Robert D. Putnam, *Bowling Alone: The Collapse and Revival of American Community.*

# My Place in the Community

What Is My Community?

Safe and Sound

Balancing Assets and Needs

Meaningful Community Connections

In the Neighborhood

A Community of Cloth

# What Is My Community?

I N THE FALL of 2011, I was a panel member in a three-part series intended to provide attendees with an overview of efforts at the country, state, and local levels to help older adults age well in a community. As I listened, I noted that everyone, including me, talked about "community." But I realized that when I used the word I didn't know what I meant by it. I resolved to figure out what "community" signified specifically for me.

There are many parts of my life and, because of this, I connect with lots of communities of varying types and sizes. These communities can be small (like my family), or big (like city agencies), or huge (like the health care system). I am linked with each of them in different ways, for different reasons, and with different intensity. In my family, for example, I am a key player, continually interacting with all members in a constant flow of talking and doing. This is a very intimate and personal community that has depths of richness and commonality. We are tied together, permanently.

I also have a lovely community of friends, but it doesn't have the same coordinated closeness as family. In a family, everyone knows each other. With friends, some may be acquainted but many may not. Some friends are long-term, some are newer, and from time to time we do things with and for each other. My friends are a loose assemblage with me as a point of connection, but they, as individuals, wouldn't see themselves as an organized group.

There is my little neighborhood where I know some people but not others. I see my neighbors intermittently—on the street, around local issues, or at holiday parties. People in this enclave would pitch in if I needed something, if I had the foresight and humility to ask.

The city in which I have lived for more than 40 years is another community where I take advantage of some things it offers (such as senior parking stickers) and try to give back by being involved in important city issues. I have made very significant connections with people who are trying to help seniors stay in our city community as they age.

I have other communities. There are geographically distant people with whom I share some common interests, not the least of which is getting older. We talk on the phone, on-line, or during visits when we try to give good, mutual advice. I have a broad (but very loose) connection to my religious heritage, but it is more in my head and heart than through any regular involvement. I do know that if I needed something either practical or spiritual I may find help there.

It is harder for me to think about big entities, such as federal and local government or health care and financial systems, as real communities for me. They are massive, mostly impersonal, and I use them when I need something very specific and limited such as social security, trash collection, medical expertise, or legal help to write a will. All are significant pieces of my expansive "community."

So, I have a multiplicity of communities, but they don't form a whole. To have a "community" that I know is there to support me in different ways I must first envision what my life might look like down the road. For example, if I can't drive, someone would have to help me get out of the house for errands, doctors' appointments, lunch dates, and other enrichment. If I am to remain socially connected, mentally stimulated, physically enabled, and visible, I must define what elements would support those intentions, and then figure out what "community" would help me sustain them. I have to be my own community system designer.

Since I know that my personal community will have to be an assortment of family, friends, services, agencies, and big systems, with a little work I can probably name them now. But before I do this I have to figure out what parts of my life I might want help with. I can do this by noticing what I do in a day, week or month. The range of possibilities is enormous—from taking a shower to going to the opera—and I have to fill in the blanks with names, relationships, and telephone numbers. Ideally my community would be a coordinated effort of a small group of people guided by one or two arrangers, who see the whole picture if I can't. It's unrealistic and possibly unfair to think that all of the tasks are the job of one person. It needs to be a team effort with me in the middle of it, and I must trust this unit to make decisions on my behalf, if and when I am no longer able.

In the past months I have learned of situations where a small group of people has come together to help someone who was finding it hard to manage on her own. In these scenarios there has been a key person who is aware of what is happening and who calls on different people to help with finances, health care, meals, health aides, and so on. They are dedicated individuals who meet informally to make sure everything is covered. This is what I would like.

An alternative would be to just let it happen naturally, by serendipity. I could hope that people would self-identify and take on the tasks of coordinator, driver, or lunch-mate. Everything might come together without my planning, but then there is likely to be an uneven distribution of responsibility, with one or two people carrying the full load. I know from experience that this is what usually happens, and I know it is exhausting physically, mentally, and emotionally. It would be so much better to do a small amount of reflection on what the future might be, identify a couple of potential coordinators, and provide them with a menu of lifestyle wants and needs, and the names of those who can pitch in and help out, when the time comes. I will rest a little easier knowing that I have done this for the wonderful people who will help me through inevitable aging.

# Safe and Sound

Over a period of a year I had a few small health problems—nothing big, but enough to nudge me (unwillingly) into understanding a bit better what it means not to feel as "safe and sound" as I used to. The first incident—a fall—left me aware of how my health status could change in a matter of seconds. I didn't sustain any injuries but was told that I should take it easy and not drive for a week. I tried to stick to these instructions. Even though I knew that my doctor was right, I couldn't follow through on the advice and began driving after three days. Maybe this wasn't the smartest thing to do, but I hated the feeling of not being able to resume my normal life.

The second incident was minor surgery that required some recovery time. "Four to six weeks to heal," they said. I didn't believe them: a few weeks; I'm a fast healer; I know myself—they don't! I was wrong, not because I didn't understand my body's quirks but because the medical system didn't take enough time to pay attention to my particularities. It took more than six weeks to feel somewhat better, and I felt fatigued and out of sorts for much of that time. During those unreal, drowsy days, I spent a lot of time listening to the radio, watching stupid television and, jolted by my unexpected vulnerability, doing some thinking about safety and soundness.

"Safe and sound," according to dictionary definitions, means free from danger or injury. In the past, I used the term and felt relief when my kids and grandkids arrived at their destination after being in a big rainstorm, or when my son made it back from a remote Alaskan island. They are home safe and sound, whew! I don't need to think about it anymore. It's over.

Although the episodes that impacted my health and well-being are pretty much behind me, they are not really over in my psyche. Unlike the relief I feel when my family is OK after a scary time, I can't feel total freedom from worry because, in my deepest self, I know I am slowly getting older and perhaps more vulnerable. This doesn't stop me from plowing along with my life, but I am somehow changed. I am a bit more cautious, more aware of my own breakability, and definitely more reflective about what it means when safety and soundness are threatened.

Like everything else, being "safe" and "sound" is very complex and has different meanings and elicits different responses depending on whom you talk to. It was a few health problems that brought me to this topic, but feeling safe and sound can apply to many different parts of my life. The list is long and just writing it down feels like planning for doom and decay. On the other hand, it could be a road map for thinking about who could help me if I should need it. In addition to physical decline, could I experience psychological or emotional problems? Could I be a target for scams? How will I manage my finances? Could I feel socially isolated and alone? There are many more questions.

This leads me to think about who I could rely on if something should happen to me again. My first layer of support is my children, although, like many aging parents, I don't want to burden them. They would get annoyed at me for saying or even thinking this, but I see how jam-packed their lives are and would prefer not to add something into that mixture. After my kids the next tier is my friends, whom I have called on to drive me home after a medical procedure. I could ask my neighbors for things like bringing me soup if I had the flu; I would just have to get over my reluctance to ask. I don't regularly attend a house of worship, but if I did, there would be people in that congregation who would come together to help in whatever way they could.

If I couldn't find close-by support from family, friends, and neighbors, I would turn to the city where I live. Like all municipalities, it has people whose job it is to help people stay involved and connected, but also to assist with sorting out problems and finding resources. I know about these benefits because I am involved in my city community. Yet it is common not to know about these services until a problem arises, and then the situation is fraught with confusion and anxiety. I am very familiar with this scenario because when my mother needed more support than she was getting at her independent living situation, I didn't know where to turn. Now I know better, and if I needed help for an older relative or friend, or even myself, I would contact my senior services department, and they would connect me to those who can lend a hand. I've learned that there is no need for me to feel unsafe or unsound; that there are wonderful people out there thinking about my well-being; and that I should not be afraid or embarrassed to call on them for help. The first chore is to get over my unrealistic attitude that I am invincible. Not acknowledging the potential for vulnerability can be a trap that prevents me from reaching out and creates a barrier to being truly safe and sound.

# Balancing Assets and Needs

I have long been intrigued by the contrasting notions of "assets" and "needs." In this instance I am not talking about tangible assets such as my house, my car, or my savings. It is more about the skills and knowledge I have that I could use for the benefit of the people around me—family, friends, neighbors, or the city where I live. When I try to make a list of these "personal assets" I get a little stuck. It takes some work to figure out what assets I have without feeling like I am patting myself on the back too much. However, there are a few pretty obvious ones, and it seems OK to mention them: I can write; help get things organized; pay attention to kids, grandkids, and older people; make presentations; learn; sew; and grow tomatoes in pots in my south-facing back yard. There are many more things that I am not good at: all kinds of technology—computer or otherwise; sports of any kind—unless simple walking is a sport; math; and growing vegetables in something other than pots.

The notion of "need" is more difficult. I don't like to think of myself as someone who requires something from someone else. I like to do things by and for myself. Identifying a need is just the opposite of back-patting. It feels like an admission of failure. But if I am honest, from time to time I may have to ask for help—a ride home from a doctor's office or shoveling icy snow when it grows to more than two feet on my sidewalks. There is another part to this needs thing. So far, my needs have been intermittent and not ongoing. I don't know if I will be able to recognize the point in time when I need routine help. So, for now, I will stick to the intermittent.

An issue that keeps coming up in the city where I live is snow shoveling. The winter of 2011 was a snow nightmare. Endless storms, record-breaking snowfalls, gigantic mounds, all of which led to never-ending shoveling. Plows piled mountains of snow onto street corners (including mine). City ordinance requires that households clear a path on public sidewalks. Even for strong, able-bodied persons the task became completely impossible in some places.

At a recent program at the local library, when groups of people were supposed to break into discussion groups about community concerns, a woman raised her hand and asked about Newton's snow shoveling ordinance. She questioned how the city could do this to its seniors, especially in light of Newton's desire to be a "livable community." This hot-button comment exploded into an intense time of questions, comments, and explanations about what the ordinance meant, who had to comply and who didn't, consequences of not complying, and how to approach City Hall—all valid concerns. In the midst of this, another woman raised her hand and said she was somewhat dismayed at the negative approach to the issue. Acknowledging the difficulty of the snow ordinance, she challenged us to think not only about what we needed from the city but to think positively and creatively about alternative solutions. Many voices expressed ideas. "Why not form neighborhood groups to help each other?" "Don't be shy in asking the person next door to help you out." "What about approaching scouting groups?" People were talking about "assets."

I live in a city that has people of all ages with lots of skills and knowledge—an abundance of personal assets. In addition to individuals, I am surrounded by institutions of learning, houses of worship, and advocacy groups. It is a great place to be. But, with all of these advantages, in my schmoozing around town, I have heard some unsettling comments. Some of them emerged in our library discussion. "My next-door neighbor doesn't care that I am home alone." "Nobody ever offers to shovel my driveway." "My old sense of neighborhood community is gone." "No one is home during the day anymore and it can get very lonely."

All of us are living through difficult economic times. Many of us are struggling to make our finances support us in a reasonable lifestyle. The people who are responsible for managing our cities and towns are dealing with the same issues, only on a much larger scale. When times were good we could expect a lot from our government, but things have changed as they, and we, have to make difficult choices about how to spend money. This downturn may actually present an opportunity for us to figure out how we can use personal and community assets to reinvigorate a sense of cohesiveness in our streets and neighborhoods. But how can we go about this?

My personal assets of sewing or writing, for example, surely won't help me deal with snow, but I could exchange these for some shoveling. I can even use my writing to promote the idea of small-scale community connectedness. My neighbors and I have talked about forming a group of some kind, but we are all very busy no matter what stage of life we are in. This great idea is still just floating around. We need a leader—and I guess I haven't been jumping up to assume this responsibility. It feels daunting. But I would love to help figure out how to assure that the people who live yard-to-yard with each other are not alone and isolated, and can get help shoveling their walk if they need it. Is there anyone out there who can begin the tiny steps needed to bring us back together by sharing our assets with each other? We could all, including me, sure use it.

# Meaningful Community Connections

Often the reason for pursuing a doctorate is to prepare for a career in academia, research, or service to humanity. When I decided to go back to school at age 64 for my Ph.D., I knew that a life in higher education or investigation was not my primary goal. I wanted to take what I learned and apply it in a practical way to help my "community." I had not yet defined what that community was, but for some reason, that didn't worry me. In fact, I was too naïve to even think of the question. All I knew was that I wanted to do something that would directly benefit people.

On the first weekend of school, the members of my cohort sat together in a circle to get to know one another. We described our interests, what kind of job we might want to have, and where we might publish our writings. Many said they would like to teach at a university and publish in discipline-specific academic journals. I said I wanted to work at the community level and publish in *Reader's Digest*. People still remember the *Reader's Digest* comment and laugh with me about it. Having such a homey goal in a university setting is not typical. In some places it would have been disdained and even dismissed as frivolous. But I knew that I wanted to bring what I learned and experienced to people who would not necessarily have easy access to or even interest in research publications. I wanted to reach anyone who might be going through experiences similar to mine and possibly help them think through their own dilemmas around getting older.

Now, ten years later, I am doing exactly what I set out to accomplish. It feels great. In general, I am working in my "communities," which I have defined with broad scope and in multiple layers. One major community is the city where I live. It has 83,000 residents, along with government, service agencies, schools, cultural resources, amenities, parks, transportation, and rules and regulations. Simply everything. In one way or another all of these elements will ultimately impact the lives of seniors because my city is on the leading edge of aging population growth. According to the 2010 U.S. Census, nearly 22% of Newton's residents are 60+ (around 18,600) compared to an average of 18.5% nationally. Seniors age 60 and over number about the same as school-age children.

A subset of my city community is my "community of readers." I publish articles in my local newspaper, and I know I have a good-sized readership because people I meet in my many places tell me they read and learn from my column. I write about the things that impact me as an aging person—from the broad societal constructs that influence how I am perceived to thoughts about how to live the rest of my life.

In addition to the articles, I am now chairperson of our Council on Aging, which is a commission appointed by the city's mayor and aldermen, and therefore an official body representing the city. Its mission is "…to serve the needs and improve the quality of life for [city] seniors." An important part of the council's mission is to advise the director of the Department of Senior Services, a city department that also reports to the mayor. How terrific to be involved in something that has such a pertinent and vital agenda. During my tenure I have become aware of so much. I have learned about Newton's older population—its talents and diversity, its contributions, and how upcoming seniors may have different requirements, expectations, and skills than previous generations. I have found out about city government—how it works and the challenges it faces balancing resources in light of residents' needs. I have been exposed to national and international trends among aging populations.

I have learned that our council and department are not alone. Most cities and towns are facing similar issues—a growing older population along with usually decreasing revenue. Everyone is talking about how to maintain important programs and services while planning for an evolving future that incorporates communications technology, social and political trends, and economic uncertainty.

Research clearly shows that people who are connected to others manage their aging better than those who live in isolation. For me, being involved in the city community serves many purposes. It broadens my world, introduces me to people I would not have otherwise known, teaches me things, and allows me to hope that I may be helping others. I see meaningful involvement in my local community as a piece of my legacy—what I wish people to remember about me. I really didn't have to complete a Ph.D. in order to be involved in this way. I could have done this no matter what my education ended up being. Yet the process of obtaining a doctorate helped me define my most important life goals and figure out how to achieve them. In fact, the achievement of a degree seems less important than my satisfaction in helping people think about their future as seniors, raising awareness about what it means to grow older in a community, planning for broad upcoming challenges, and, most personally, creating connections that are meaningful to me in the city where I live.

# In the Neighborhood

My little neighborhood has a medley of houses from three eras: Victorian—big, embellished porches; post–World War I—rectangular, no-nonsense adornments; and post–World War II—practical, smaller. These are the landmarks by which I orient myself each time I step outside. They are comfortingly familiar.

I know a few things about those who live in the houses around me. I know where there are young children, empty nesters, or elders like me. In the past few years my neighborhood has blossomed with kids who live in houses previously occupied by seniors who no longer wanted the responsibilities of maintaining a home. Both the houses and neighborhood have shifted from one generation to another, and each change has generated gain and loss. While new neighbors ensure that houses are filled with future dreams, old connections can disappear, leaving only fragile memories of what it was like in the past.

Since my street is only one block long, during the warm months kids are on the street with scant worry that cars will interrupt their play. From inside my house, I hear the thump, thump of a basketball on pavement, the grinding sound of skateboards on sidewalks, and sometimes, the unintelligible chatter of young girls deep in discussion in the next yard. These sounds tell me that people feel safe here.

I know that the people who live around me are kind and caring. I am asked to holiday parties, and my grandchildren are invited to run under sprinklers when they are with me on hot summer days. My grandson loves to sit on a stone wall and watch the big kids shoot hoops. In discussions over our shared fence, my neighbor and I talk about complex and simple life issues: how to create a new path after retirement or the colors of our newly painted houses.

I have to admit I am a lazy neighbor; I connect mainly with people whose houses I can see out my windows. It wasn't until I went around with a flyer explaining my renovation plans that I met some neighbors who had lived here for as long as I had. In my 20-minute foray to nearby streets I met an editor who gave me advice about publishing; learned about an upsetting land controversy; and heard stories about the difficulties of helping older people make decisions while avoiding intrusion into their private lives.

This last issue hits home for me. On the one hand I want to feel attached and connected to my neighbors; on the other hand I like my privacy. As a proud person, I especially don't want people to be concerned that I need help when I see myself as an able, active, competent older adult. In thinking about this I realized I had to figure out how to handle this tug between openness and seclusion. My sustainability in the neighborhood depends on it.

Almost without realizing it, I have been drifting in the direction of disclosure as I began to share things about myself, not privately, but in a public way. After I wrote an article about some minor health issues, my terrific neighbor across the street left a plant at my back door with a little note saying "We love having you in the neighborhood." Can't do much better than that! It is curious that I didn't share my health episode directly but tossed it out there for anyone, including strangers, to know. In retrospect, it seems that by speaking publicly I shielded myself from having to reveal anything personal to any individual. I am pretty sure I didn't publish the article in the hopes that someone would respond, but it is quite lovely that one of my neighbors did. Maybe next time I am faced with some difficulty I will have the courage to speak directly and frankly to those who live around me every day.

Participating in a neighborhood takes work, especially when people are of different ages. Because of a common life-stage, families with young children may have an easier time communicating with each other. Those without that shared experience may slip away from core neighborhood awareness. Since neighborhoods are dynamic, relationships can be hard to maintain. But if the notion of neighborliness is to succeed, then at least some of us must open ourselves up to sharing in a meaningful way. This idea got me thinking about what to do if I needed help with a household task. The first and hardest step would be to admit that I couldn't do it myself and be up-front with my neighbors about my need. Perhaps if I could figure out how to contribute back, then it might be more acceptable to ask.

Having had this insight, I constructed a series of questions. What can I contribute to my neighborhood? What kind of help might I need? How do I communicate these "assets" and "needs"? How can neighbors communicate with me? How do I help them and how can they help me in a reciprocal way? There are no simple answers, but the only way to figure out how to sustain my close-by relationships is to tackle the questions one by one and start talking to the people who live around me. We will learn something new and perhaps begin the process of knowing how to support each other, respectfully, in the neighborhood.

# A Community of Cloth

In my basement I have a big plastic chest with four deep drawers. This is where I keep odds and ends of fabric that I have collected over the years. Some of these pieces of cloth are left over from projects, like covers for sofa pillows or an occasional dress for a grandchild. Others are simple purchases that I acquired just because, at the time, there was something about the patterns that reflected my mood or created a feeling of mystery. I bought these materials in different places, and after each foray, I brought them home and tucked them away in my stash figuring I would create something fun, practical, or even exotic—someday. But in the 20 or 30 years that these remnants have been in my possession they have sat there unused. I would look at them from time to time but I always put them back, uncertain about how to make them into something meaningful. Over the years they lost a lot of importance because I had forgotten why I got them in the first place—although I do remember some feelings of tenderness at their purchase.

I am at the stage of my life when I am trying to clear away stuff and am slowly working through my closets, shelves, and dressers to discard things. But the little bits of fabric in my basement always present some small challenge. It is easy to know what to do with old clothes, books, and trinkets. Local charities always welcome them. But I haven't been able to figure out what to do with the fabrics. "Who could possibly want them?" I would ask myself. There isn't enough of any one piece to make something big, and none of the remnants match. It would be hard to put them together; they are so very different in style, touch, color, and weight. Each time I looked at them, I could not come up with an answer, so I would refold them and put them away until the next time I took them out.

Then an opportunity presented itself. I decided to go to Cuba—a very foreign place for many Americans (including me). One of the few ways that U.S. citizens can go to Cuba is on a group educational, humanitarian, or religious tour. I signed up for a mission to visit several struggling Jewish communities and bring items that they have trouble obtaining—simple things like toothpaste, underwear, and pencils. I asked our tour leader if any special things were needed, especially for the new senior center at the Centro Hebreo Sefaradi, one of the three synagogues in Havana. "Use your imagination," she said. "Hmm," I thought, "maybe they like to sew. Maybe they could use some fabric." With vague hope, I stuffed some small pieces into my already full suitcases—lightweight cottons; colorful blues, purples, and greens; unusual patterns with birds and flowers. I packed as many as I could even though I had no idea how they might be used.

It wasn't until the very end of my trip that I had the chance to visit the center and see the seniors' handiwork, some of which they sell to visitors. Along with decorated Stars of David, I saw challah covers—decorative and symbolic cloths used to cover the loaves of challah, the braided, eggy bread so integral to the Jewish Sabbath meal. I bought one made of plain cloth with simple embroidery—a reminder of my journey to Cuba. Maybe my scraps of cloth could be used to make challah covers and sold to well-wishers like me who are anxious to make some contribution to this isolated Jewish community. Visitors might bring these reminders back to their homes around the world and use them to celebrate the Sabbath with their families. I can fantasize about a network of disparate, detached pieces that are part of a larger combination of meaning and practice that is scattered around the world in an infinite variety of colors, sizes, and textures. I have formed a mental image of a floating and shifting composite of odd, separate pieces which, together, reflect the fabric of Jewish diversity around the world.

Now that I am home, I am thinking again about my dresser, which remains quite full of a colorful array of fabrics. I still don't know what to do with them, and they could sit idle with no meaning for another span of years. But…my imagination is prodding me…if I had a way to get them into the hands of people who can sew cloth and create challah covers, these scraps could become treasured items for use in Jewish homes and, perhaps more importantly, for paying homage to those who struggle mightily to keep Jewish practice alive in remote communities that few of us even know exist.

Other people must have their own pieces of fabric tucked away, waiting for a purpose. What a vision—a community of cloth. But I am just daydreaming. For now, I can only hope that the pieces I brought to Cuba will become something Jewish and end up as personal reminders to other visitors who are unknown to each other, citizens of many places, but virtually all together in a community fabric of tradition.

The house is not an object,
a "machine to live in";
it is the universe that man
constructs for himself...

—Mircea Eliade, *The Sacred and the Profane: The Nature of Religion*

# My Place in My House

Our Houses and Our Dreams

Continuum and Transitions

Should I Stay or Should I Go?

What to Do with My Stuff?

# Our Houses and Our Dreams

I HAVE AN INTIMATE relationship with my house. This place, with its straight walls and boxy windows, supports and surrounds me with stability and comfort. It is small and sturdy—it suits me. I feel safe in this familiar house, knowing all the ins and outs of living here—the tucked-away spots where I can stay warm in the winter; how the sun shines through the back windows in the late afternoon; and the funny noise the pipes make when the washing machine is on the spin cycle. I know what causes that sound and I know not to be afraid.

It has taken me many years to understand this house well, and I take care of it so that it will continue to shelter me. My house is full of memories, shaped by my perceptions of what has happened here—the countless family events, gatherings of friends, and holiday celebrations. Objects clutter my space. Framed artwork on walls, photographs on tables, and old furniture that I inherited from people I love are all suffused with memories.

My house and the things that fill it up have become a complex entity. I have overlaid life-defining significance onto this structure and its contents.

Some of this meaning reflects the phenomenon of the American Dream, which propelled people like me to strive for financial stability, retreat from cities into suburbs, educate children well, and own a home of one's own—a symbol of independence and self-sufficiency. So many of us did this, and so many have stayed. Today, one-half of Americans 65 years and older live in the suburbs, often in single homes. Dreams about our houses become personal as we superimpose reveries about the past, present, and perhaps the future. In *The Poetics of Space*, Gaston Bachelard says the "chief benefit" of a house is that it "shelters day-dreaming, the house protects the dreamer, the house allows one to dream in peace." (p. 6)

I often wonder how long I should stay in this house. My thoughts bounce randomly from one extreme to another. Maybe I should move to a place where I don't have to worry about shoveling in winter. Maybe I should stay and make arrangements for people to come in to deal with all contingencies. Maybe I should just wait and not create stress for myself right now. After all, I am still self-reliant. In my many talks with older persons like myself, I find that I am not alone in these musings. All of us at this stage of our lives face these concerns, and they can present momentous dilemmas about what to do.

Even if I think tentatively about different staying or leaving scenarios I am instantly confronted with daunting questions. If I want to move, where do I go? What situation will suit my needs and desired lifestyle? How do I fit my accumulated stuff into a smaller space? How will I meet people I like and trust? How do I pay for a new living place? If I give my things away, who will remember their meaning?

If I should decide to stay there are different questions. How can I find people to maintain my house, inside and outside? How can I arrange to have space for a live-in to care for me? Can my house earn money to help pay bills? If I decide to wait and see—to stay "as long as possible"—the main question is when will I know that it is time for a decision? What must I consider in order to know when the end of "as long as possible" has arrived?

The decisions about whether I stay, move, or wait and see are as complicated as the life I am accustomed to living. Just thinking about a potential decision makes me ponder what my house means to me and who I am as its inhabitant. It forces me to deal with the physical, social, and emotional involvement I have with the place where I live and to look at what's ahead.

The questions can be endless and intimidating. Just framing them can stop further thought. For myself, I have found that when faced with difficult deliberations the best thing to do is start with the mundane act of gathering information. I find that much of the time I am fearful of tackling dilemmas because I don't know the choices available to me. I don't know how to begin. Getting informed could be a safe way to reach beyond the invisible barriers I have set up for myself. New knowledge will broaden my understanding of what's available in the world around me. Perhaps it will lead to a decision, a fresh way of thinking, or nothing. It is up to me. I need to decide how to use that learning. No matter what, I need a place to live in that lets me continue to create dreams.

# Continuum and Transitions

When I talk to people about where they want to live as they get older, many say "I want to stay in my house for as long as possible. I am not ready for a nursing home." This comment intrigues me, perplexes me, and makes me sad.

It intrigues me because it reflects our reluctance to acknowledge the long process that lies ahead between now and some undefined future point in time. It is as if one day we are healthy, competent, and functional, and then on another day, without warning it's nursing-home time. There seems to be a mental leap over perhaps a few decades of living to an imagined precipitous landing in an unhappy end-of-the-line place. Yes, the time may come when we are not able to manage on our own, but what really happens between now and then?

I have been an observer and a participant in the process of aging. I cared for many loved ones whose lives came to natural ends in nursing homes. These were vibrant, self-sufficient, life-loving individuals who I never thought would be unable to take care of themselves. Yet, they became disabled and dependent. It was so difficult for all of us. But it wasn't an all-of-a-sudden thing. It happened over a span of many years during which they lived in houses, moved to new apartments or independent living facilities, and looked for ways to redefine themselves. It was only after several transitions and at quite advanced ages that a nursing home became the only option.

The comment "not ready for a nursing home" perplexes me. Experiences with my elders who made it into their 90s before they became incapacitated reflect the path for the majority of us.

Only a small percent (4.5% in 2000) of people 65+ are in nursing homes. And in fact, that percentage is declining, with the biggest drop among those 85 and older (18.2% in 2000 compared to 24.5% in 1990). Perhaps we only hear the "bad" stories, but our perception that the only choice after a house is a nursing home doesn't reflect reality. The vast majority of us seniors are in the community in various types of living situations.

Sadness enters in for me when I think about people who may be living in fear when there are options and so much living to do between now and the end of "as long as possible." Perhaps holding on to our houses when they become too difficult to maintain may prevent us from exploring ways of reinventing our lives. Maybe the question should not be "How can I stay in my house?" but a series of questions such as:

"How do I want to live my life in the years between now and then?"

"Does trying to maintain my house lead to more stress than I want to deal with?"

"If I move from my house, will it free up some physical and emotional energy to be used in creative discovery?"

In my regular musings, which I try to do objectively and without fear, I imagine my life as a continuum to be navigated over the next 10, 15, or 25 years. Instead of thinking "no nursing home," I have decided to put my energy into envisioning a list of potential next steps and roughly the points at which I might think about reevaluating. For example, I can stay in my house for 5–7 years, find ways to know my neighbors and community better, and locate people to help with routine maintenance.

After that, I could sell my house and rent an apartment, or buy a condominium nearby and stay another 5–7 years. No worries about shoveling, and I'd be freed up to investigate new avenues that I didn't have time for because of house responsibilities.

Or, I might consider an independent living or a "continuing care" community where there are things to do and interesting people to meet, but probably not until age 85 or so. Some of these places have affiliated assisted living and nursing homes, which can provide an easier transition, if necessary. Personally, I'm not afraid of a nursing home (assuming it's a good one). The idea of having people around me 24 hours a day whose job is to take care of me when I can't is quite comforting.

I know that moves are stressful, but making at least one in the next few years might result in freedom from burdensome chores. It could help me figure out what to keep and what to get rid of so my kids won't have to deal with the unnecessary stuff I have accumulated. And, it could prod me to be imaginative about my life.

There are options to ponder as I go through this journey and it is up to me to decide what's best. I believe that the stark, good/bad comparison between living independently in a house and deteriorating in a nursing home is not only false, but instills a fear that prevents us from being proactive about the future. How better it is to think about a continuum of living with mindful, creative transitions, over which we have control.

# Should I Stay or Should I Go?

Like so many people my age, I wonder whether I should stay in my house or go someplace else. It has taken me years of investigation and deliberation to understand this complex, thorny issue. In my learning journey I visited rentals, condominiums, and "continuing care" communities. Each had advantages and disadvantages ranging from convenient or isolated location, abundance or dearth of options, beautiful or dull surroundings, not to mention big variations in cost. These forays helped me understand my choices and define a list of things to consider when, and if, I decide to leave my house.

Most of my journey was not through visits, though, but in my mind. Sitting in my living room, driving my car, shopping, or walking in Cold Spring Park, I would think about staying or going. I pondered my house's positive and negative qualities. Still, after all my efforts, I continued not to know the best way to think about it. "Why is this so difficult?" I wondered. One reason may be grounded in the American Dream, which instilled all of us with notions of home ownership, independence, and control— now embedded in how we define the very essence of who we are. But there must be other reasons. Knowing that my title for this article was the same as a 1980s song by The Clash, I printed the lyrics for "Should I Stay or Should I Go," not really thinking that it would give me any clues. I am not, and never was, into punk rock, yet some lines popped out. "If I go there will be trouble, an' if I stay it will be double." There it was—my immobilizing quandary! Indecision, the song suggests, traps me—holding me back from the rest of my life. If I stay, my situation may be comfortingly familiar but detrimental to my well-being. If I leave, I could be liberated but experience frightening losses. "This indecision's bugging me. If you don't want me, set me free," the song continues. Our houses can't make decisions to release us from their clingy embraces. But we do have the power to consider what our houses offer us and challenge their characteristics if they are not meeting our needs. We are in control—not our houses.

People I talk to about staying or leaving fall into three categories: determined to die in their own beds; willing to move; or waiting. I fall into two categories—not opposed to moving, but waiting. In the meantime, I am taking some action.

My house is a small ranch. The washer and dryer, a small make-shift bathroom, and my office are in the finished basement. The main floor has two small bedrooms, one 1950s pink and gray bathroom, and narrow doorways. For years, I had been thinking about what I could do to age in my house safely and comfortably. I made up fantasy drawings and graph-paper plans. My biggest problem was deciding if I should renovate or sell. The house is in a great location: a friendly neighborhood, near public transportation, and within walking distance of one of my city's small village centers. It has good bones and does not require much maintenance. The negatives are a lack of room flexibility, stairs, and fading appearance. Acknowledging that I wasn't ready to make a decision to move, I chose to work on the things I could fix, only needing to decide how much to do and timing. I knew what I wanted (all those fantasies and plans) and took to heart what my dearest friend says: "If not now, when?"

This is what I've done so far: painted the exterior; enclosed an underused porch; put in another main-floor bathroom with a washer/dryer hook-up; and widened some doors. I will work on other things over time. I did the renovations based on many "ifs." If I have a walker or a wheelchair, I need to get through doorways. If I can't carry my washing up and down steep stairs, I should have a laundry on the main floor. If I don't want to work in my basement office, I can move it upstairs. If I need people to live in, there is a bedroom for them and privacy for me. The work cost me more money than I expected. I rationalized the expenditure by saying it will help me age in a known place; it may be cheaper to have a live-in caregiver than go to a facility; and it will make the house more sellable, especially to an elder who wants to live in a cozy little house.

Everyone's situation is different, and each person needs to decide what is best for her or him. But we all need to do some mulling and planning. Having done this work, I feel a little less stuck. It has been a creative adventure. I recommend it.

# What to Do with My Stuff?

I have too much stuff. Over the past year or so I have been trying to clear away some of it to freshen up my living space, and also to increase the likelihood that my kids won't have to deal with it when something happens to me. I have thrown away old files from old projects, clothes that I haven't worn in ten years, bits of paper with messages that have lost their meaning, and a few disintegrating books. There have been several stages of getting rid of things. First was the decision to tackle the job, second was going through items to determine what to keep and what to toss, and third actually transporting them to some final destination. So far, most went into the trash.

Even with all of this work I still have files to go through, more clothes to sort, and books to discard. Of all of the stages of clearing out, the longest was clearly the decision to do it. In my case, it took years. I spent a lot of time thinking about it and then putting it off for many reasons—not enough time, routine and special events, social obligations, daunting task—whatever. When I finally put my mind to it, going through the items to find those with special meaning ended up being the second longest task—maybe a few months. Throwing things out took days.

We all have things: old photographs, letters, defunct legal papers, souvenirs. Although a nuisance, it was worth spending the time because I found things I never knew existed, like the legal papers when my father changed his name because he couldn't get a job with the one he was born with, or a letter written by my mother to her children, that she never sent, which made it clear that any money she had was for her own use until she was dead.

This sorting and thinking took time, and no one could do it but me.

I've been thinking that the stuff surrounding me is my own cache of artifacts representing the bits and pieces of my unique personal culture—almost like an archaeological museum collection, although most of my things have little, if any, value except perhaps to explain family history to my children and grandchildren. However, most likely they won't have the inclination to piece together the complexity of my existence but will only want to keep things that involve significant memories for them.

In the November 7, 2011 issue of *The New Yorker*, James Wood's article "Shelf Life" brought the issue of "stuff" home to me. He writes about trying to determine what to do with his father-in-law's massive, unsellable book collection and says, "And though my task was easy compared with my mourning wife's, the experience made me resolve not to leave behind such burdens for my children." Through the process of cleaning out the books he realized that, "The more time I spent with my father-in-law's books, the more profoundly they seemed to be not revealing him but hiding him, like some word-wreathed, untranslatable mausoleum." (p. 43)

Wood clarifies and connects two important issues. The first is the desire not to burden children with the job of sorting through and deciding what to do with things left behind. This is the practical piece. The second has to do with the value of handing down a comprehensive and comprehensible picture of the person who has died. This is the heritage piece; it is about explaining the persona and context of a past life. The two issues are intertwined because it is not possible for descendants to decide what's important to keep without the background story. Over the next months I will do more tossing, but this time I will identify what past episodes are important for my kids and, ultimately, their kids to know, and identify the relics that will help tell the story. I must gather items and explain them in my words to create a mosaic of heritage. This would include the August 1925 articles in Boston and Woburn newspapers about my grandmother, who was acquitted of bootlegging (even though she really was selling illegal alcohol), and the newspaper photo of my great-grandparents celebrating their 75th wedding anniversary in 1931.

I want this compilation of my life's fragments to be small enough to fit in a large plastic storage container that could easily be tucked into someone's closet. I will write explanations on little pieces of cardboard to describe the importance of each item and to make connections to other pieces—like the notes on objects in a museum. By doing this I will reveal a picture of me as a whole person in the context of important people and events that surrounded or came before me, and influenced who I am today. Someone going through the plastic container would gain a straightforward and non-mysterious view of me and my heritage in less than an hour or two, which is more than enough time to spend at my museum of one.

No road is long with good company.

—Turkish proverb

# My Place Among Family & Friends

### Part I: Earlier Generations

### Part II: Contemporaries

### Part III: Future Generations

# *Part I: Earlier Generations*

### Resilience of Memory

### A Caregiver's Reflection on Atlas

### Beyond Crying

### End-of-Life Decisions

## Resilience of Memory

I STARE AT THIS photograph. It stubbornly prods me to revive old memories. The image is of my father's family. It is 1916 and they are standing in their yard in Wilmington, Massachusetts, surrounded by objects of domestic life—pots, pans, laundry and, improbably, a stove. My dad, Louis, is in the picture (that nice-looking boy on the right-hand side), maybe 12 years old. His sister Minnie, about 10, stands next to him, her big smile and boldly striped apron foreshadowing the confident young woman she would become. Next to her is Lena, shy and holding tightly onto a puppy. Young Joe is in the front, looking a little sheepish. My grandfather, Nathan, stands behind them, his cap creating darkness across his face; next to him is Bessie, the oldest child, partially hidden by her father's shadow. My grandmother Rebecca, looking much older than her 40 years, is holding the baby, Eddie. You can't see his face—only a mass of hair. Here they are: all of the Goldbergs together.

The memories scurrying through my mind are not really mine. I have expropriated them and made them my own. They are hand-me-downs, and I put them on like a used outfit that has been passed on to the next child in line. These memories spring from the stories I was told growing up, embellished over the years by my imaginings of what life must have been like back then. Aunt Lena, Uncle Eddie, and my father told me the stories, each in their own way and voice, and I listened. I have woven them together to create my own understanding of the collective story.

The Goldbergs were poor. They spent their early years as itinerant peddlers, roaming the Northeast on a horse-drawn cart as my grandfather earned money to feed the family. He was a seeker, looking for the new place, the new scheme, the new life. Their migratory life meant that the children were born in different places—some in Maine, some in Massachusetts. Eventually, they settled in Wilmington, a few miles north of Boston, where my grandfather had bought a wooded plot after a chance encounter with a land speculator. It was time, he thought, to get a regular job, settle down, and build a house in the country where his wife could raise chickens and grow vegetables, and their children could breathe fresh air and go to the same school each year. Nathan was a powerful bull of a man. He chopped down trees to make way for a house; my father and Minnie, both strong and vigorous, helped out. They created a squat, square, black palace from felled trees, old lumber, and tarpaper. They drilled a well, constructed a chicken coop—the largest anyone had ever seen— and built an outhouse, shed, and stable. I know all of this because of the stories.

I look at the picture again. Everyone seems content. Some are even smiling. Looking at this photo, you would never guess that the family's dream of a permanent home was short-lived. Shortly before the picture was taken, loose material near the oil stove caught fire and the new place burned to the ground. My grandfather managed to get everyone out in the few horrifying moments before the house was incinerated. Knowing what had happened, the photograph describes a different story: the family is standing in the yard of their burned-down house—the pots and pans, laundry, and stove are all that remain from the devastating fire. With nowhere else to go, the family moved into the chicken coop and cooked outside where it was safer. Yet, amid all the upheaval, the family took a few minutes to gather and pose for an unknown photographer.

Despite the fire and living in a hen house, life was still better than it had been during the years on the road. The family had property, eggs, and vegetables. There were six healthy children, a new house almost completed, and the security of my grandfather's job at a tannery in Woburn. I look at the picture again, knowing that the future wouldn't leave them secure for long.

To get to work, my grandfather had to walk from the house to the railroad yard in Wilmington and then take a train to Woburn. Early in the evening of September 16, 1918, as the family sat in the kitchen, a dark-suited man walked up to the house and told my grandmother that her husband had stepped into the path of a moving train. His legs had been severed. I don't know the details of how it happened. My understanding of the story is based on the memories of children who were concerned with effects, not causes. Their father was dead. He was 48 years old. On the day of the burial, for lack of space in other vehicles, my father had to ride in the hearse. He was haunted all his life by the memory of his dead father lying in the coffin next to him and wondering, as a child would wonder, if his legs were in there too.

I look at this photograph and try to imagine it without my grandfather. I see my widowed grandmother with her six children, the youngest just three years old. With some railroad compensation money they managed to get through the next few months. The older children tended the chickens and garden, and accompanied my grandmother into Boston where they sold eggs. She accepted donations of coal but doggedly refused handouts of food.

In 1919, the year after the accident, Prohibition was legislated. Rebecca, with some gentle coaxing from a few friends, saw an opportunity to maintain her family without accepting charity. She began to make and sell bootleg whiskey and blueberry wine. For the next six years, people came to the "tavern in the trees" to buy hooch. Some of her best customers were prominent citizens—judges and policemen among them. She knew her regular customers and was wary of new ones. Always alert to a trap, she would interrogate newcomers in her broken English. "Who sent you? Who are your friends?" In 1925, hired "spotters" implicated her in the illegal sale and keeping of liquor and she was arrested. The defense counsel, in a highly unusual move, called the chief of police (one of her customers) to the stand as a character witness. Rebecca was found not guilty of both charges.

With profits from the sale of eggs and alcohol, the children grew up, graduated from high school, got jobs, and began to earn what money they could during the Depression. Bessie went to work for ten dollars a week. Minnie started an antiques business. My father went to college and graduated—an extraordinary achievement. Lena got a job in Boston but lived at home. The family settled into another period of relative calm.

More stories flow out of the photograph and remind me that by 1940, Minnie, Bessie, and my grandmother had become memories, too. I was born a few years after Minnie had died in childbirth, and my parents named me for her. When I was 13, I inherited her gold signet ring with her initials, MG, engraved on top. I would sit for long hours tracing the intricately intertwined letters trying to determine where one ended and the other began, imagining what Minnie had been like—a beautiful woman celebrating life.

My father, Lena, Joe, and Eddie are the only Goldbergs from the photograph that I knew. Bessie, who had uncontrollable diabetes, and my grandmother died within months of each other when I was about two. Eddie, who was the last one to survive, talked about the family often. When we looked at this photograph, he said that maybe his face was hidden on purpose so that he wouldn't see all the tragedy that was coming.

Family photographs are misleading. They tempt you to think that one frozen moment can sum up lifetimes, but the picture is merely a catalyst; it's the stories that add flesh to the images. With each piece of my family's history this picture becomes more fluid and alive. It is possible to imagine a vital and vibrant Minnie, a strong and determined grandmother, eight people living in a chicken coop—the rich, complex layers of routine lives.

This family did whatever it had to do to survive. They trudged through their lives with some help from family and a few friends, but mostly they did it on their own. It is not amazing, incredible, or admirable. They did it because they had no choice. After each catastrophe, they gathered up their lives and kept going. With hindsight, we might call this resilience, but I don't think they would have seen it that way. I think they simply knew how to get through each day, to move on after tragedy struck, and to celebrate times of calmness and joy. When they got together, they would retell the family stories—each one a lesson about when to laugh, when to cry, and how to keep going. The stories bound them together, just as they bind me to them.

So, yes, the family could be called resilient. But what is truly resilient in the Goldberg story are the memories. The few keepsakes that I have—some newspaper articles, old photographs—are infused with them. They are carved into my consciousness as deeply as the letters MG are carved into Minnie's ring. My father and his family transferred these powerful memories to me through their stories, where they remain stubbornly alive. I feel obliged to tell them to my children and, perhaps someday, to my grandchildren. Maybe these stories from the past will be strong enough to last in the memories of another generation or two. Maybe my own story will be added to them. I'll never know, of course, but I am compelled to try. It is my way of showing respect for my family's persistence and for the power of story to create deep, irrepressible, resilient memories.


This essay was first published in the 2003–2004 edition of *Whole Terrain*, Antioch University New England's literary magazine. It was published under the pen name of Leah Majofis.

# A Caregiver's Reflection on Atlas

I have been a caregiver for numbers of loved ones. Most were old, and all were unable to care for themselves towards the ends of their lives. During these "watching over" years, I made forays into diverse and unfamiliar places and struggled with frightening uncertainty. I took on these jobs not understanding where they would take me, how tough they would be, and the intensity of assault on the core of my being. Each circumstance was different and filled with emotional contradictions—sadness and joy, anger and love, fear and enlightenment. As I took care of these people, I managed other things—work, school, family—too many tasks with a scarcity of time. Simultaneously, I felt supported and cared for, yet alone and lost. Although others tried to help with a few parts of what seemed a puzzle with infinite pieces, I was the one handling countless, disorienting events. (Mom needs photo for DMV handicapped sticker. Oh no! Can't park in handicapped spot—no sticker yet. Parking space too narrow. Can I get her heavy body into wheelchair?! Can I push her through chaotic lot without being hit by crazy driver?!)

My experience was not unique. I am one of millions who has assumed the job of caregiver. Each of us can describe this journey in words, but language alone can't express how it feels. I remember a sunburst of insight on one particularly difficult day. "Wow, this is what Atlas must have felt like!" I thought, relieved that I had discovered a potent image for that all-consuming task of caregiving. I'll try to explain.

First, though, sit down or stand in a quiet place. Close your eyes. Imagine you are Atlas—that forsaken Greek god-figure who was tricked into carrying the whole of the universe for eternity.

Feel that enormous, seething load pushing down on your shoulders as it compresses your body so you can barely move. Experience the fierce ache in your arms as you try to keep stable the gigantic package. Realize that you can't ever move from this spot, because if you shift your position some important piece could tear off and barrel away. Look forward (that's the only direction because you can't turn your head). You see an object speeding towards you and know that you should pay attention. But you agonize, "Should I try to capture it and shove it into this living mass, or should I let it rush by and say, with resignation, 'I'm already doing the best I can with what I've got'?" You assess the situation and know that if you try to grab the object, you will stagger to reestablish your precarious balance, and in doing so you might drop something and feel badly about it. There is no winning and little peace.

I don't know if the Atlas metaphor reflects your experience—symbols are personal—but it worked for me. His challenge provided a context for a responsibility that I did not comprehend before I took it on. It helped me understand the physical and emotional complexity of a circumstance where you are all at once in control but paralyzed by conflicting options and demands.

Through the years as I cared for people, I wondered why it felt so hard. After all, birth, living, and death are parts of normal human progression. Ultimately, I realized that taking care of the frail was difficult partly because I had no experience, no intimate role models to seek advice from, and even if I did have someone to go to, I didn't know what questions to ask. It was hard also because medical, social, housing, and transportation systems were uncoordinated. Each interaction with one system led to follow-up somewhere else, resulting in more work and confusing answers.

Finally, it was hard because sometimes I had to make decisions that may have contradicted a relative's wish. I tried to make rational choices, but even so, there was usually a heavy burden on my conscience.

In spite of the hardships that caregiving brought I am grateful for having done it. It helped me understand the process of aging, how systems do or do not work, how decision making is not a straightforward path, how each situation and person is unique, and, most importantly, that those who care for others need endless compassion. I would not have given up this experience for any other. It broadened my knowledge and helped me clarify who I am. Unlike Atlas, my responsibilities had a natural ending from which I could move forward, having learned more about living (and dying) than I could have ever imagined. I am thankful to have gained a little emotional wisdom which is now permanently and profoundly etched on my spirit.

# Beyond Crying

The other night I had dinner with a longtime friend. We try to get together once a month to catch up on our lives, our kids' lives, and anything else that is on our minds. This time she told me that, just a few weeks ago, she had moved her mother, who is in her 90s, into a nursing home. My friend was plagued with sorrow, anxiety, and guilt. She was totally worn out and it was palpable. One of the strongest feelings of shame came because, as she said, she was "beyond crying." "What's wrong with me?" she said. "I can't cry."

How can it be that through all the strife of making and then carrying out this decision she couldn't cry? She felt it was unnatural, but it wasn't. I know because, as I told her, I too couldn't cry over that long, long period when my mother went from independent living into a nursing home, when she declined over three more years, and when she finally died. In fact, although I tear up from time to time as I think about my mom and all of the great aspects of who she was, I still haven't cried.

I remember vividly when I decided that it was time for her to go into a protected environment. It had become clear that she needed 24-hour care with people to help with most parts of her life—prepare her food, make sure she took her medications, provide some social connections, and pick her up if she fell. The decision to act came quite precipitously. It wasn't that the situation shifted dramatically or abruptly. My mother didn't all of a sudden get worse. It was simply that she couldn't soldier on any more and neither could I. Although I didn't provide all that she needed, I was the one in the relentless, day-to-day caregiving. I had the main responsibility for thinking and worrying about what could (and did) happen to her, and then dealing with the unhappy aftermath of multiple unnerving events. I had agonized for a long time, and then one morning I just decided.

Once the decision was made I concentrated completely on finding a place, selecting what to keep and what to give away, distributing her furniture, moving her, and not looking back. The time had come for her, but more importantly (some might say selfishly), it was time for me. My emphasis switched from trying to sustain our current situation to a focus on the future. The future for her was inevitable, ongoing decline—but now in a safe place. Her safety had become the predominant motivating factor. Just as compelling was my acknowledging that, if I were to take care of her, I also had to take care of myself. I knew that I couldn't continue the physical and emotional strain.

Over the next three years in the nursing home, my mom continued to decline. She became more and more separated and isolated even though she was surrounded by good people. Her physical condition confined her to a wheelchair, her hearing loss prevented her from having conversations, and the deaths of dear family members left her drained and withdrawn. This all happened gradually, almost inconsequentially; some things were hardly noticeable. Nothing to really cry about—only sadness at the inexorable process.

I was with her a lot—visited her almost every day; sang songs with her and anyone who wanted to join in; and wrote down the words of other residents and put them into a book of poetry.

I didn't cry during all of the decisions and transitions. Probably I was too emotionally exhausted. I didn't consciously prevent myself from crying. I wasn't being stoic. It just didn't happen. When my mom died, I called my brother and sister, my sons, and other family members. There were few others to call because she had out-lived most of her contemporaries. I made the arrangements, answered questions, and cleared out much of the remaining shreds of her life. With the exception of a few photographs and a little bit of jewelry everything else was thrown away. The steps seemed prosaic and mechanical. At her funeral, not only did I not cry, I didn't speak. I felt that everything I might have said had already been said to her—through words, but also through the years and days and hours that I spent trying to make her life as comfortable and meaningful as possible.

So, maybe that's it. Perhaps my expression of caring had already manifested itself mainly through deeds carried out in love and admiration for her. In her own way she let me know that she appreciated my efforts, and that felt good. I couldn't cry and I didn't need to cry. Her life was over, and mine was moving forward. And besides, she probably would not have wanted me to cry. That was just who she was. So I write this for my friend and others who are taking care of loved ones. It is a hard road cobbled with unpredictable emotions, and I want my friend to know that she isn't alone, and that it is OK not to cry.

# End-of-Life Decisions

Over the course of ten years I made end-of-life decisions for three unique individuals: my mother, my aunt Lena, and my cousin Fred. I was the health care proxy for all of them. In spite of good care, thoughtful interventions, and supportive environments, each was on a path towards dying. Frailty was the only thing they had in common.

It's easiest to start with my mom because hers was the simplest decision. My siblings and I knew her well enough to anticipate her wishes with certainty. After having lived independently until her early 90s, she entered a nursing facility because she needed 24-hour care. She signed a do-not-resuscitate order. At first she seemed to adjust—talking to people, participating in activities. But most of the time she just sat—waiting. Over three years she became less engaged and more inert. Then she stopped eating. I figured she didn't like the food, so I made special things. But when I presented the fork she clenched her mouth shut. One day I offered egg salad (her favorite) and she slapped my hand away. Stunned at her aggression, I finally realized it was her way of telling me she was ready to die and I needed to let her go. It was her decision—not mine. So I stopped trying, and together we waited quietly until she died peacefully a few weeks later.

Lena was different. The same age as my mother, she was determined to live. When she was 93 I admitted her to rehabilitation after she became dangerously thin and was constantly trying to undress. She refused to sign a DNR order. The medical staff suggested that I sign. My two adult sons said I should, but her sister-in-law Celia said, "Lena would want you to do everything to keep her alive." What was I supposed to do? Here was a woman who wanted to live, and I had to decide if I could honor her wish. But Celia called back with a gift of trust. "Lena probably would not want to live in that condition," she said, "and besides, it is your decision, and I will support whatever you think is right." The next morning, as I was leaving to sign the DNR, the doctor called to say that Lena had died during the night. She spared me the act of signing but not the agony of the decision.

My cousin Fred, just a few months older than I, began having seizures when he was a toddler. Epilepsy was poorly understood in the 1940s, and treatment was largely an uncharted field. No matter what therapies were tried, Fred continued to seize, fall, and suffer head injuries, which in combination, ultimately limited his capacity to understand complex issues. In his late teens, when his parents could no longer take care of him, he was placed in a state hospital where he lived for about 40 years until the Department of Mental Retardation's de-institutionalization policy moved him into a group home. When Fred's parents died, his brother Arthur took over responsibility. When Arthur was dying from cancer I told him I would watch over Fred.

After a few years, Fred began to aspirate food, resulting in multiple hospitalizations and debilitating pneumonias. Fred never had a legal guardian, but his care team suggested that I become his health care proxy. The law requires that, without prompting, an individual must name someone to make decisions in the event that they are not able. The problem was that Fred couldn't understand what that meant. He kept saying he would make decisions for himself. Finally, with several witnesses present, he named me as his decision-maker. There were only two medical choices—a feeding tube or not. I wrestled with what his parents or brother would have done and consulted with his niece. But, ultimately, I decided not to order a feeding tube, knowing that it wouldn't prevent ongoing problems. Hospice was brought in, and after several pneumonias, Fred died at home among friends.

Three people—one who wanted to die, one who wanted to live, and one without the capacity to make reasoned choices. Making decisions for someone close to the end of life can be daunting or relatively simple. It depends on whether thoughtful planning and communication occurred well before the approach of death. I learned, through hard experience, the necessity of naming a proxy and providing enough information so that she or he can decide with as little anxiety and guilt as possible. I experienced the ordeal of making a decision contrary to someone's wishes. Most importantly, I discovered the power of trust—a gift that only we can give to those who will carry out our own end-of-life decisions.

# *Part II: Contemporaries*

## Junior Debs

I GREW UP IN the 1940s and 1950s in Providence, Rhode Island. I always knew that I lived in the less desirable part of the city—South Providence, as opposed to the East Side where, in my mind, everyone had a lot of money and was kind of snobby. My friends and I were just down-to-earth girls with parents who were struggling to make a living. Of course, as I got older I realized that nearly everyone's parents worked hard to maintain a family home, but as a child I believed "they" were rich and I was not. The girls on the East Side belonged to a Jewish sorority that had a tradition of never allowing South Side girls to pledge. Maybe it was because many of them belonged to a country club that my friends and I saw them as "debutantes." In this era of social and ethnic rankings the idea of Jewish debutantes was a wacky incongruity, but that was our perception.

By the time I got to junior high school, a small group of us concluded that we wouldn't strive for membership in that heady milieu but would form our own group. We called ourselves "The Junior Debs"—and still do. The origins of our name have become murky, with each of us having a different version of the story. Unlike the East Side girls we kept our group simple. We didn't have an initiation or enrollment process—whoever tended to hang out together automatically became part of our little band. We got a big kick out of raising our questionable status up to one that had immense significance to us and essentially being able to say "screw you" to the East Side girls (although we would never have used that language but rather "the heck with you"). Some of us even vowed never to join that unwelcoming sorority, if they should ever ask.

We formed the Junior Debs around 1950 when we entered the seventh grade. There were about thirteen of us. By the time we got to high school we were a pretty cohesive group. Then the unthinkable happened. The East Side sorority opened their stuck-closed doors and asked us to pledge. It was historic. The "Debs" spent hours debating whether we should join or reject the offer. Do we want to be part of that scene? Do we want to go through a demeaning initiation process? What would that do to our Junior Deb status? Should we join just to show we are as good as they are? In the end, there was no consensus. Some Debs joined and some did not, but it was not without a lot of heartache.

Through all of this and in spite of the diversity in affiliations, the Debs kept together for six years, which was a long time in a teenager's life span. We did some community service, had a few innocent '50s-style parties, and folk-danced. Mainly, I think our purpose was to just be part of a group of people who had known each other for a long time and who shared some common sense of togetherness. When we graduated from high school, most of us went to college. Some of us left Rhode Island and some stayed.

There were mini-groups of Debs that kept in touch, but we lost our collectiveness.

Then one day, Harriet, my longest-term friend from across the childhood street, called me and said, "You know, we will all turn 50 in 1988," (I knew exactly who she meant), "and we should have a reunion." The Debs hadn't been together for almost 32 years. We didn't even know where everyone was. She and I began calling the people we were in touch with and finding people who had been out of our consciousnesses for decades. Every person we called said "YES!" The enthusiasm surged through the telephone lines.

Several of us decided that the reunion should be in our home state, and Fredda, Rona, and I booked a bed and breakfast in Newport. Everyone we talked to showed up—from 20 to 3,000 miles away. It was quite amazing. We spent hours and hours in daytime and nighttime catching up—32 years of catching up. We talked endlessly about our parents, siblings, spouses, children, houses, work, interests, joys and losses, what happened to us after high school and college, marriages, divorces—everything. The B & B owner got annoyed at us because we were up so late laughing. Around midnight, Elaine knocked on the door of the only room that was not occupied by a Deb to ask if someone would take a picture. A young man with only his boxer shorts on said yes, with his female roommate staring sheepishly from the messy bed.

We decided to meet again in five years, and since then we have been meeting more frequently, knowing that untoward things can happen in between our gatherings. We have come together in places all over the country and have photos of what we all look like as we get older and older. And indeed, throughout these years there have been many changes. Three Debs have died, as have parents, siblings, even children. There have been divorces and moves. Some are still working, some have retired. Occasionally, we bump into people who say that they were Debs too but no one can quite remember.

We are coming up on our 75th birthdays in 2013 and will be reuniting yet again. This time, though, it will be a little different. We have decided to find a setting where we don't have to do a lot of walking, searching for restaurants, or slogging around places of interest. Maybe a cruise. This is quite a decision for our active, curious, and intrepid group, but we will be there because where we go is not the important part. It is being together that matters. We are bonded by a shared, long-ago experience when we felt quite proud to not fit the mold and to declare ourselves an independent little band with a unique identity, all within the narrow boundaries of our 1950s world.

# When Harriet's Mother Died

Harriet's mother died when we were not quite seven years old. I have wondered, all these years, why I always say "we were" instead of "she was." Maybe it is because we were such close friends, intimately connected by location, time, and circumstances, and now, as adults by shared memories. When we were very young, we lived diagonally across the narrow city street, each on the first floor of a three-family house. We had been born within hours of each other though we didn't share a birthday. We still love to tell people that we are only a few hours apart in age—she was born on July 31st before midnight and I just a few hours later on August 1st. We were childhood friends who played together, talked together, and shared intimacies. Every weekday we walked the more than a half-mile back and forth to school—even at age six. In the 1940s we were in school in the morning, came home for lunch, and then went back for the afternoon. Mothers didn't have cars to drive us and fathers were off trying to earn enough money to pay the rent.

Kids in the neighborhood walked together for friendship but also to create a fragile sense of security. Our blocks-long trek down Oxford Street to Lexington Avenue School took us through a menacing gauntlet. We were Jews in a hostile environment. On one side of the street there was an orphanage, a convent, and some church buildings. On the other side there were some smaller buildings and the huge St. Michael's Church. We walked past these buildings four times a day. It wasn't the buildings that were so scary but the kids who would stand on the steps of the church taunting us with anti-Semitic epithets—"Jew Bagel," "Dirty Jew," "Christ Killer." They stopped short of physically attacking the girls but would sometimes beat up the boys, and they threw snowballs at all of us in the winter. Maybe this was another reason that Harriet and I kept so close. So small and vulnerable, we must have felt some reassurance just by being together.

We weren't sisters, of course, but I remember feeling that we were sort of like sisters—even perhaps twins except we didn't look at all alike. She was tall with long, blond hair and blue eyes. I was small with straight, dark hair and dark eyes. I was a little envious of Harriet because of her blond hair and blue eyes, but also because she had a grandmother and grandfather, and I had neither. She would visit her grandparents, who appeared to love and protect her. I wondered what it would be like to have someone like that whose house you could go to for something extra special. A few years ago, Harriet sent me a picture of the two of us with her grandparents. Other relatives were in the picture, including her dad George and several young men in military uniforms. Harriet was next to her dad and I was in the front wearing a babushka. Neither of us was smiling. It must have been taken in 1943 or 1944—maybe a year or so before Harriet's mother died.

Our neighborhood in South Providence was mixed—some Jews, some Catholics, and some Protestants. Mainly, though, the Jewish kids played together, usually in the streets, and in all seasons. There was no room to play in the cramped two-bedroom flats. In the summers we were in the city playground next to my house—on the swings or in the sandboxes. In the winter we built snow houses and snowmen, and then came in to the warm kitchen where our mothers hung up wet, heavy wool snowsuits to drip-dry near the stove.

In a neighborhood like this, everyone knew what was going on. In the summer with the windows open you could hear people yelling or children practicing music. We all made jokes about Toby Aronovitch's violin. Other times adults hid secrets from children and discussed them in soft tones. It was a time when people didn't speak openly of illicit affairs, gambling habits, disease, or death. Most of the time I only knew that something grown-up was going on by the way my parents talked quietly in the evening while I was falling asleep in my bedroom so close to the thin kitchen wall.

I remember events from that time—often simple little things like the time we made a snowman on the street in front of my driveway and it got so big we couldn't move it away. I remember feeling a little scared and guilty when my dad came home exhausted and couldn't get into the driveway. He had to demolish our snow barrier before he could come in to get warm and eat dinner. I remember the eeriness and emptiness as I looked out our kitchen window during a polio scare when the city had closed down the playground shower where flocks of neighborhood kids usually cooled off in the hot summer. I remember how we all laughed when in the winter my mother stood up the frozen pants that she had just taken in from the clothesline, and how they slowly melted and collapsed in a puddle on the floor. In my house we came in through the back door, into a little hallway and then into the inviting kitchen with my mother always there, always present, always with us. These are sweet and poignant memories, but none of them had the impact of what happened the day when Harriet's mother died.

Harriet's house was always a little quiet. If her mother was home, and not in the hospital, she was often not well, so it was important to be quiet when we were inside. Harriet's flat was much like ours. I remember coming in her front door through a little entryway and into her living room where a china cabinet displayed dark red goblets behind glass doors. I remember being captivated by the color, which added mystery to what I thought was a somber place.

On the day that Harriet's mother died it was warm and clear. It was an ordinary walk home from school. We were probably talking about the usual things that six-year-olds talk about. And then everything suddenly and violently changed. Sheldon had gotten home from school before us, early enough to hear the dreadful news. In this tight little Jewish community, news, especially bad news, leapt from house to house within seconds—friend to friend, across third-floor porches, from street to street. When Harriet and I reached the corner of Croyland Road and Oxford Street, Sheldon was there waiting and then shouting in a taunting, sing-song voice… "Harriet's mother's dead! Harriet's mother's dead!" It was not a nameless boy hurling Jew-hating epithets at us. It was someone we knew. Those few seconds of Sheldon's nasty verbal assault were instantly iron-branded into my consciousness. I remember hating him with searing anger. Still, after 65 years, the intensity of that moment has not diminished. I still feel it and sometimes cry a little when I recall it. I remember the horror I felt as Harriet darted ahead of me and I ran to follow her. I wanted to catch up to her but couldn't, and by the time I had gotten to our street she had already disappeared into her house. When I got home—into the kitchen—my mother told me it was true.

I must have known what death meant, even at that early age. I knew that it was bad and permanent. I knew that it was something to feel awful about, and I remember feeling awful. They say that it is typical for children whose friends lose a parent to worry about their own mothers and fathers dying. I may have thought this, but what I remember is the pain and sadness I felt for Harriet. How terrible it must be for her. I wanted to comfort her, to be with her. It may have only been for a few days, but it seemed like a long time to me when they took Harriet away to be with her grandparents. She seemed to have disappeared. It was a loss for me—not seeing her every day, not having our routine school walks and play time. I wanted to be with her to give my six-year-old's comfort, and I couldn't.

In all the years that we have known each other, Harriet and I talked only a little about her mother's death. I wondered for decades if I should tell her what I recalled, concerned that I could raise difficult memories. I questioned my motives if I told her what I remembered. Would it be to get that disturbing memory out of my mind, or would it be for both of us to reach back in time together? Finally, I decided to tell her what I remembered. How precious it could be, I rationalized, if she knew that I remembered that dreadful moment. After all, she and I had already talked a great deal about our memories, ones that only she and I could know, like when she broke her leg and I sat with her to eat a home-packed sandwich in a restaurant near school because she couldn't walk back and forth for lunch. This one was different though—more intense, more intimate, and deeply personal.

It was in the fall of 2008, shortly after our 70th birthdays, that I told Harriet what I remembered—the moment when Sheldon shouted at us as we walked home from school. When I told her, she stared at me and shook her head saying, "I don't remember." She had no recollection of that instant that was so overpowering for me. Her memory was that she went home, where her father and other relatives told her about her mother and said she was up in the sky. She remembered going to her grandparents' house, which was only about a block away. She remembers nothing of observances around a funeral or a shiva.

I wasn't with Harriet during those days immediately following her mother's death. I don't share her memory of what happened on that day just as she doesn't share mine. My expectation of having common recollections about that trying time, I now recognize, was somewhat of a fantasy. Logically, I know that each person chooses what she remembers and the way in which it is remembered. In spite of this mature reasoning, I was bewildered by Harriet's reaction. Her not remembering made me wonder about my own recollection. Did this really happen? Could I have misinterpreted the event? I have thought about this for many years and have resolved to accept my memory as it sits there in my heart. I don't think I could have imagined it—too many specific details about time, location, person, and circumstances. I can't reject my memory. It is too much a part of my spirit and will remain embedded forever.

What I have finally realized is that our friendship is not diminished by the lack of a shared memory. It doesn't matter that her details of that day don't match mine. What is far more important is that I was there at the time of her mother's death. I remember her great loss and even now feel very sad for her when I think about it. Harriet and I are bound by our long friendship and many memories, just not the one of that fractured moment on the street. We now live distant from each other and try to connect as much as we can. I feel tied to her in a way that is different from any other friendship and believe that I still have the right to say "we were" not quite seven when Harriet's mother died.

*Dedicated with love to Harriet Ann Diamond Adelberg*

# Sibling Complexity

My writings, when arranged together, reflect a loose assemblage of experiences and emotions that represent the multiple but interconnected aspects of my life. Each essay describes a happening of which I have been a part either through design or serendipity. One of the most complicated chunks in this free-flowing arrangement is the one that relates to my siblings. This situation of siblinghood has these same characteristics of both intention and chance: it was my parents' desire to have three children, but it was by chance that they produced such singular individuals.

I have written about previous generations, future generations, and even my own contemporaneous friends, but to create a complete picture, I had to write about my siblings. I struggled with this writing task more than any other. It was impossible to know where to begin and even how to frame an approach. Everywhere I started was fraught with complex thoughts and emotions. This is to be expected. After all, we have spent anywhere from 67 to 73 years sharing parts of our lives. I finally realized that even to attempt an understanding of my complicated reactions and feelings, I had to begin with some basic facts, hoping that this would help get me closer to sorting out the difficulty I have in writing about us.

I have two siblings. My brother, Arthur, is two years older than I am and my sister, Paula, is seven years younger. Arthur's memories of me started, most likely, when he was four or five years old. My memories of Arthur probably began at roughly the same age, and he was always part of my life. Both Arthur and I remember Paula's birth in the middle of the summer of 1945 when WWII ended, and when our mother was in the hospital for about a week. It was a strange time not having our mother around, but also not knowing what having a new sibling would mean to our family. I did sense that things would be different in some way. I guess a lot of attention was paid to this new baby sister, but I don't remember much since I was out playing with my friends a lot. Our tiny two-bedroom flat got more crowded. Paula was in the crib in our parents' bedroom. Arthur and I continued to share a room until he was 12 and I was 10, and it became obvious that with his approaching teenager status, that was no longer a good idea. In addition to our parents, there were two other tangible things that all three of us shared—the crib, with the decal of Little Bo Peep, and the high chair with two little terriers. I still have these pieces of children's furniture even though they were considered not safe even when my own kids were little.

There are things that we three don't have in common. As children and now adults we were, and still are, quite different from each other. We look completely different, have different personalities, and live in different places. We share a few memories from childhood but these, in reality, are just fragmented recollections of growing up together, particularly with Paula, because she is so much younger. Certainly we lived with our parents in the same houses until we left home. But when we talk about our childhoods our remembrances are disparate. Arthur and I remember the three-decker next to the scruffy playground, with our formative years spent on a narrow, kid-filled street. He and I recall the difficult financial times, playing outside in all weather, being acutely aware of the threat of WWII, the polio scares that kept us indoors, and our parents singing in the kitchen. Paula did not experience this time and place. She was born as the war was ending—only three years old when we moved to a nicer three-decker on a street that had trees. Her childhood time was one of less fear in the world and a somewhat better family financial picture. I don't know if she had a community of friends close by that could gather together on the street as Arthur and I did. I was too involved in my pre-teen life to pay attention.

Arthur knew my friends and I knew his because often there were siblings, like us, who were close in age. But with a seven-year age difference, my friends were not Paula's friends. Yet, even though Arthur and I knew each other's friends, our friendship worlds were disparate. Girls and boys rarely did things together except when it was winter and snowman-making time. I played with dolls and tea sets while he did mysterious things in hidden places with the other boys. Paula shared none of this with us. In some ways, she grew up as an only child of what was considered, in those days, to be older parents—37 and 41 when she was born. Paula and I didn't spend a lot of time together as children. When I left for college, she was only 11 and was not quite 13 when I married and was gone for good. We were separated in time, era, and, therefore, memories. She was of another generation.

Of course, as we all grew into adulthood, the age differences didn't seem to matter so much, but by then we were already divided by big distances and distinctive life experiences. We tried to see each other as much as possible in brief summer visits or family celebrations, and we talked long-distance. But for much of each year we were quite separate.

As adults, we share some similar values, such as a love of learning and the arts. But the connections and interactions among the three of us are not simple, partly because of unshared memories, the divergence of time and space, and gender. Added to these elements are our individual personalities, which have made for a great deal of relationship complexity. No matter how hard I may try, I would not be able to explain our complicated bond. We do care and worry about each other, talk as often as we can, and know a lot about what is going on in each other's lives. Much of what we talk about now is our own aging. We have entered into a common process and are experiencing many similar dilemmas.

But above everything else, the major thing we have shared is our parents. They did everything they could to make us ready to exist in an adult world given who we were as individuals. Quite simply, having common parents is the binding factor for our siblinghood. Since I can't explain our relationship in a multitude of words, it seems the simplest form of poetry expresses the complexity of being siblings.

Three of us grew up

Into divergent pathways

Same parents loved us

# Talking to Melissa

I first met you, Melissa, about nine years ago. We had both come to Antioch University in New Hampshire to attend an open house for prospective Environmental Studies Ph.D. students and somehow, in some random way, we found each other and talked. Our interests and experiences were vastly divergent—from different places, different eras, and different backgrounds. We were almost 30 years apart in age. Yet I remember liking you immediately. Maybe it was because I sensed your curiosity. You talked passionately about your commitment to endangered Atlantic salmon and wanting to protect and improve their habitat. You asked me what I hoped to study and I said I wanted to understand the aspects of the total environment in which people live. "Oh, I never thought about the environment in that way. That's cool," you said. That impressed me—your honesty, acceptance, and openness.

Just from that brief encounter, I hoped that you would enroll in the program, and I was excited when I saw you again on the first day of classes. We spent the next few years gathering knowledge and collecting insights—each of us in our own direction but with constant back-and-forth learning. I learned so much from you by watching, listening, and just knowing you. I noticed how you created your own path, your determination and skill, your deep, multi-layered character, your sincerity and caring, and your great personal strength. I respected you immensely. I saw you as a good, thoughtful friend and still do.

When I got the phone call telling me that you had died I couldn't absorb it. It was without warning, beyond comprehension, and totally unthinkable. I remember that it was a beautiful warm, sunny day, and I went to look at the ocean hoping for some solace. It didn't come.

Some people may believe that when a person dies the essence of their physical and spiritual being is transported to a place that none of us can see. It is a place that can only be imagined, but where people live in peace. In this place there is much hoped for calmness and love—for eternity. Others may believe that a person's spirit hovers around the living and even guides them as they move about in earthly places in daily routines, through joy and struggle. Still others may believe that with death a person is just gone with stunning finality.

I cannot, nor do I wish to, debate views of what happens after death. I cannot even say with any certainty what I believe. I only know what I feel and sense. Melissa, I can't envision your spirit as something external and separate, existing in some other place. Nor do I think you are hovering and guiding me. Also, I can't accept that you have just completely vanished. When you were alive, and as I got to know you, I felt that I was absorbing some of your essence. You embodied the spirit of nature. What I feel now is that elements of you are here in me, under the surface. My thoughts about you seem to be stimulated by simple, natural things that I experience through my senses. I feel your sensitivity when I touch the smooth surface of water-washed stones on the vast, duned ocean beach where I walk in solitude. I experience your energy when I see the brilliant sunlight create vibrant iridescence on the foam of the ocean waves. I hear your voice when the birds, whose names I don't know, waken me at dawn. And I remember your intensity when I taste the first sip of cold white wine as I watch the fiery, orange sun set behind the trees beyond my deck.

I do not project your life-force out there in some imagined space, searching for a peaceful spot to settle. These images are too abstract for me. I can only see, feel, and experience your presence in something that I know well. That something is me. I do believe that people who have died continue to live on in people's memory. For me, though, it is more than remembering your image. It is about the feelings that I experience when I conjure up a picture of you in my mind. Your essence has become a part of me, and I carry you along with me in my feelings every day and every moment and will for as long as I am aware of who I am.

*In profound and respectful memory*

*Melissa Laser, 1969–2010*

# A Continuum of Friendships

I have layers and layers of friends. Some I have known from very early childhood and others I have met quite recently. My longest-term friends are ones with whom I can share ancient memories. We are bound together by collective early circumstances. We grew up in the same era, had similar experiences in our youth, knew each other's families, and, in some ways, were forced together in friendship by the way the dominant cultures of the day defined who we were. It is possible to describe our early life happenings to others, but unless someone had been part of our social grouping early on they would absorb the words in their intellects, but not feel the emotions we carry in our hearts. So in this regard, old friends have very special, situation-specific characteristics that can't be replaced or found in newer friends. Having said this, there are also people I knew as a child but with whom I have not sustained a firm friendship. A few of them I may see at high school reunions, but mostly they are not part of my existence now. I guess we didn't have other qualities like compatible personalities to hold us together.

In my relationships with many old friends we talk about our memories. But these are not the only things that keep us connected. Throughout the decades, and now as older women (most of my old friends are women), we have discussed all the varied dimensions and aspects of our lives. We can do this because we have established a certain degree of trust over the years, but also because we have enough similarity in worldviews and values to make trust possible.

As I think about all the things I discuss with old friends, I realize that I talk about the same things with newer friends.

Depending on when someone came into my life, there may have been one dominant life theme that became an entryway for creating friendship. For example, as a young mother I found a few friends as a bunch of us were dealing with our children's growing up. As a working person, I found colleagues who eventually became friends. In going back to school as an adult, I established strong connections with people who were, like me, scrambling to finish advanced degrees. I have even become friends with some of my teachers and advisors. Some of my most profound connections came through being a caregiver. I became bound together in compassion with others who were doing the same thing. It was by sharing this realm of anxiety and stress that I realized that no one who had never been a caregiver could truly understand what it was like.

In all of these situations, I and those plodding through the same issues with me were learning, laughing, weeping, agonizing, and creating new memories. This kind of exchange had happened with many of my older friends, but it continued to happen with the newer friends I met along the way. I expect that this will persist as I keep moving into different phases and places in the future. My life is not static and neither are my friendships.

I now see my friends, not in the rigid categories of old and new, but as a continuum of friendships that keeps building over time. They have blended together into one large flowing organism. While it is critically important for me to retain long-term relationships, I have to keep my eyes and spirit alert to the potential of new and emerging friendships. The older, middle-aged, and younger people I meet may be nearby in my neighborhood or city, or anywhere in the world. Things are different from when I was a child. The cultural boundaries that limited my personal interactions have broken down so that I now have the freedom to find acquaintances wherever I want. I know this because it keeps happening. Just as with older friends and more recent friends, it will take a while to know the potential for building that all-important trust. This is the primary and most profound component. I must always work to be a trusted person, and I hope that a friendship will not end because I lost trust in someone or they have lost trust in me. That continuum of friendships will keep me going for as long as I have the strength and foresight to sustain it.

# We Are Living Our Futures Now

I was a casual planner for much of my life. A lot of my early planning revolved around what was expected—do well enough in high school to go to college (even though my studies didn't prepare me to earn a living), marry, have a family, live in a house, maybe work at some kind of job when my kids were old enough…and then what? My planning didn't involve much thinking and what little there was didn't have a lot of depth and substance. Mainly, I just let things proceed with little intervention on my part.

It wasn't until I was around age 50 in the late 1980s that I began to realize that serendipity wasn't necessarily the best way to let the future happen. As a newly single woman, I had few savings and not a whole lot of marketable skills. I owned a small house but had no idea how to sustain it over time. It was then that planning became foremost and I set out to achieve two goals: afford a decent place to live and not be poor when I was old. Fortune and luck continued to play an important role, but I became much more deliberate in taking advantage of promising opportunities. I got involved in organizing local political campaigns and, as a result, was offered a job based on my previously unknown or unacknowledged (by me) organizing capabilities. Over the next years, I gained more skills and knowledge, and finally garnered enough self-confidence (and salary) to know that I could live in a decent place. Goal number one was accomplished.

The second goal—achieve some financial stability—required a much more conscious effort. I made the assumption that I would be my own primary support —it was up to me and only me. I had no idea where to begin but found an early-morning adult education course on financial planning for women—inexpensive, easy to get to, and good timing for a working woman.

This course ended up being a defining episode for my planning. It wasn't even the whole hour that was significant. It was a one-second statement: "Pay yourself first!" the instructor said. "You have to pay your bills, but you must consider yourself the first payee. Pay yourself first and then pay your other bills. You won't miss that money and you will secure your future." That very day I arranged to make the maximum contribution to my employer's matching retirement fund. I know these perks are not so common any more but, at that time, it provided me some peace of mind and lessened my worry about being old and poor. Second goal accomplished.

That was almost 25 years ago. But once I achieved those two goals I allowed myself to drift along feeling somewhat secure—even with the recent awful economic downturns. In the past few years, however, especially since I turned 70, I slowly began to realize that I needed new goals. I had become complacent and reluctant to think about what my life would look like as I continued to age. There wasn't the urgency of 25 years ago, but I know from experience that circumstances can change in an instant. Yet I continued to think that I could wait until tomorrow.

Finally, after fighting powerful inertia, I renewed my planning. Some of my goals now are similar to those from before—around where and how to live, for example. But I added some new objectives that are more reflective and realistic because my challenges are different now: How do I continue to lead a meaningful life? And how do I define what help I might need down the road?

One on-line definition of the word *future* says "time or a period of time following the moment of speaking or writing..." I like this. It says that the future can be as short as one second away or as long as infinity. For me, it begins when I finish this article. Each time I complete something my future starts anew, and what had been the future becomes something accomplished. This means that I am already living my future, and I need to hurry up and plan realistically right now for what could happen tomorrow. If I don't, I am allowing serendipity to take control of my life again.

# *Part III: Future Generations*

### Legacy

### A Birthday in the Context of Memories

### You Can't Always Get a Chocolate Croissant

### My Sons in Paintings

# Legacy

THE OTHER DAY I bumped into a friend at the supermarket. After checking in with each other, he said, "You should write an article about legacy." I jotted the idea on my shopping list (I have many scraps of paper with ideas to explore) and proceeded to tell him that I thought this was a complicated topic with many dimensions. "Hmm," he said, "I was thinking about finances."

He's right, of course. It is essential to document our assets and wishes, making it clear what should happen if we become incapacitated and when we die. If we don't do this while our minds are competent, we risk at the very least confusion among beneficiaries. Besides, dealing with these thorny issues now means that we have some control over this tangible part of legacy. Having acknowledged this, my mind shot off in tens of directions. Yes, finances, but what else?

While driving home, I mulled over what I wished to leave my children and grandchildren. I reflected on what my family passed on to me. Certainly there were physical items—my mother's little gold earrings, my father's songs, my aunt Lena's Art Deco ring, my aunt Gert's washboard—each emblematic of distinctive temperaments and complicated lives. But my musings kept coming back to intangible things—much of it related to my mother.

My grandparents were immigrants, and most died quite young. My parents, who had siblings that died from accidents, diseases, and poor medical care, went through childhood and young adulthood in the early 20th century when the Depression devastated lives. During their marriage my father did hard physical labor, and when my younger sister entered junior high school my mother decided to go back to work, even though my gentle dad objected strongly. His reputation as a provider was at stake. "I want my own money," my mother responded. "If I want to have lunch with a friend or give some gifts I don't want to have to ask your permission." He acquiesced.

When she died at 95, their small estate was divided among their three children. The inherited money was lovely, but the memory of my mother confronting my dad about her sense of worth and independence, at a time when this was uncommon for women, was profound.

My mother's strength keeps popping up in odd ways. As I was cleaning out my house, I found a letter that my mother had written but never sent, saying essentially, "any money in my accounts is to be used for me and not for the benefit of my children until I am dead." Throughout her life she was generous—financially, when possible, and emotionally, always. She loved and encouraged us, admired our talents, knew our faults, and was, most of the time, very accepting. Why she felt the need to write down her strong preference and why she never sent the letter will remain mysteries forever, since none of us were aware of the letter's existence until I discovered it after she died. However, her words and wishes were not a surprise because they were totally consistent with her brave autonomy and clear-mindedness. These qualities formed the foundation of her legacy to me.

I would be arrogant to think that I can mandate what my children should value about me, and I am certain my mother had no conscious intent to influence my memories of her. Just as my brother and sister have their interpretations, I know that my kids will, over time, define my legacy to them according to their own remembrances and unique personalities, which is as it should be.

For my grandchildren, though, I feel a bit more prescriptive. At the simplest level, I want to leave memories of a grandmother who cherished them. I had no good experiences with grandparents. Three died before I was born and the other was mentally ill. When people say how lucky I am to have grandchildren, I respond by saying it is far more important that they have grandparents. So, I hope my grandchildren will remember affectionately our everyday, pleasant times together. But in addition, I hope they will be able to conjure up less tangible aspects of my character that could guide them, just as my mom's strengths inspired me. This is my imagined bequest as I have constructed it so far, and I will continue to revise it over time as all of us, together, continue to get older.

I will pass on a few concrete items that I hope will prod my children's and grandchildren's reflections and help them think about what they would like their own legacies to be. But, if I find that I have things to say that may be uncomfortable to talk about, I will try hard to raise the issues while I am still alive rather than write a letter that they would only read after my death, when it would be too late for understanding and resolution.

# A Birthday in the Context of Memories

My birthday is August 1st, and every year I reflect a lot around this time. Last year's thoughts were particularly intense because my older granddaughter, Hannah, turned seven, and it triggered powerful memories. The summer I turned seven was a defining time for me. It was 1945 and World War II was ending. My recollections of preceding years are of war preparedness—air raid drills, soldiers, sailors, rationing, and blackened headlights. But that year, when the world was consumed by news of wars in Europe and the Pacific, my main concern was the impending birth of a sibling.

My mother knew that she wouldn't be home on August 1st because the baby was due to be born in late July. In those days, women spent about a week in the hospital after delivery, so she planned ahead. First, she made sure I had a present. The two of us took the bus downtown and climbed the stairs of a seedy building to a second-floor jeweler to pick out a Star of David for a necklace. I remember sensing that having this symbol was a step towards being grown up—old enough to take on responsibility. She made it clear that it was my choice, and I selected a small gold star with raised edges. I felt proud of my decision. Over subsequent years I wore it a lot and still have it tucked away in my old jewelry pouch. From time to time I take it out and look at it—especially during the summer round of birthdays.

The second thing was that she and my dad, together, decided to send my older brother to camp for a week (he was not happy about this) so as not to have two kids to worry about while my dad was at work. A neighbor watched over me during the day, but I didn't like her and tried to avoid her as much as possible. Mostly

I was insulted because I believed I was capable of taking care of myself. I could play with friends in the playground, go inside and make a sandwich, or rest if I got tired. I can't remember if I complained, but I do know that I was annoyed that no one saw how competent I was. After all, my mother trusted me to pick out my own gift.

Often, I take long walks to figure out what I am trying to get at in my writings. This time, as I ambled I realized that my feelings were not about sentimental longing or nostalgia for a simpler time. Nor were they about sadness for everything that has been lost between then and now, or even pleasure in all the good things that have happened. Most assuredly, they were about shaping my concept of who I was at my core, even at age seven.

I am always surprised when I recall my strong feeling of competence at that young age, particularly because it took many years for this sense of self to re-emerge in my adulthood after being hidden for decades. Why it became concealed, I don't know. Someday I will explore this, but for now I only acknowledge that it faded away without a clear explanation during my teens and young adulthood.

More importantly, I wondered how I could use this memory to consider who I want to be as a mature adult—particularly as a grandmother. This brings me back to Hannah. I wondered what her concept of herself is at age seven. Does she have a good idea of who she is at this young age? I can watch and observe how she confronts the world, but I can't really know what she feels and experiences. That will be up to her to explain whenever she is ready. However, I do know that whatever its shape, there is a depth of understanding and awareness within her. I know because I was once seven. I remember what it feels like, and because of this I know how important it is to respect the inner thoughts and feelings of a young child. When I am with her, I try to encourage a sense of self-worth, wanting her to sustain it, unbroken, over time. That is my gift to her for the past, for now, and for the future.

# You Can't Always Get a Chocolate Croissant

### (Acknowledging Mick Jagger)

I have two sons, two daughters-in-law, and three grandchildren. The first episode of the chocolate croissant saga was on the day my grandson, Sam, didn't eat any breakfast. Early every Tuesday morning, I go to my close-by daughter-in-law's and son's house to help my two older grandkids get ready for school. I usually prepare their breakfast and make sure they get dressed, brush their teeth, and organize their backpacks. I then drive them to school. I have been doing some kind of regular childcare routine ever since my granddaughter Hannah, now eight, was a baby. When Sam was born, I kept doing the same thing—usually on Tuesdays.

On this particular day, I dropped Hannah off at school and then proceeded to take Sam to his preschool. Right before I was to turn into his school's driveway, I asked Sam if he was hungry. He said yes. Conveniently, there was a Panera's just down the street. We went inside and I asked Sam what he wanted. "A chocolate croissant," he said. I immediately cringed and panicked a little—what had I gotten myself into? Too sweet, too filling, too carbohydrate-filled—not a good choice for a kid's breakfast. I tried to convince him that he should choose something else, but he was adamant. I caved.

The second episode in this saga happened that same afternoon when I collected Sam and then picked Hannah up from school. Sam told her that he had a chocolate croissant for breakfast. "What?!" she said, "When am I going to get a chocolate croissant?!" A perfectly reasonable thing for her to say, but I kept putting her off. "One of these days. Sometime. Not sure." Over many months I lost track of the actual number of references to the chocolate croissant, but there were a lot. Sam kept bringing it up, and Hannah kept asking when she was going to get one.

At some point, I realized that I had to figure out a reasonable response that would put the croissant discussion behind us. Finally, after much deliberation, I understood what the real issue was, and it had very little to do with pastry. It was about how I needed to define what was fair and equitable for them and for me. The dilemma had to do with the extent to which I could provide identical things and experiences to each of my grandchildren so that they felt they were getting equal attention from me. There was no way, I ultimately realized, that I could guarantee equality. First, trying to assure that each child got the same thing put me in a position of constantly having to catch up—a no-win situation for me. Second, it could give my grandchildren the impression that there was always something due to them from me—an unproductive and inhibiting situation for them. Third, and most importantly, it denied the reality that each of them was an individual with a special personality, growing up within different times and spaces. Because of this, I could never give them the exact same things. My gifts and my relationships with them would be, and should be, different.

My job and responsibility is to figure out how to support each of them as they continue to grow, and to find the right, personal thing. If I am successful, these will not be totally "equal" but fair and appropriate for them, and only for them. I will try very hard to get them what they need, which may not be exactly what they want. Looking at it this way helps me and them know that they are each important and special in their own way.

I have explained this to Hannah and Sam and think they understand, but if they don't now, I expect they will in the future. My third grandchild, Lina, is only a baby (five months old at this writing) and she, too, is an individual with her own persona. Using the lesson that nothing can be exactly equal, I will define my relationship with her when she gets old enough to ask questions. I am pleased that I have figured this out now so I can respond to her personal uniqueness and help her develop her distinct path. Hopefully, all of my grandkids will determine what they need, and as much as possible, I will help them get it. Fairness will be my guiding principle, not equality.

# My Sons in Paintings

In my house I have many paintings. Most of them have a story behind them but two stand out as very special. In both paintings the main subjects are my two sons at different times and ages. The first is pastel and watercolor. It was created sometime between 1976 and 1978 and shows four boys dressed in hand-made colonial outfits, carrying American flags, and steadfastly marching through an undefined background of earth and green. The story of this painting has three phases—before, during, and after—all of which occurred in Wellfleet, on Cape Cod.

It began in July of 1976 when there were preparations all over town for the Bicentennial parade. My sons Philip and Daniel and my two nephews David and Joshua were together at the Cape. I'm not sure how it all started, but since Philip was almost eleven and the oldest of the group, it was probably he who convinced the other boys to walk in the parade. David was eight; Daniel and Joshua were seven.

I remember the flurry of activity as the kids made paper tri-corner hats, a coffee-can drum, American flags, and obtained a plastic fife—all of which were to be used as props to depict the famous painting, *The Spirit of '76*. There was a lot of excitement as the planning and creating went on. On the morning of the parade, the kids tucked their pant legs into their socks to simulate Revolutionary-era britches. We brought the boys to the starting line and then selected a location where we could watch their progress, and be very proud.

The second phase was the parade itself, which was full of patriotic fervor and attracted thousands of people from all over. The kids walked with great determination, although the younger ones began to slump after about a half-hour in the hot sun. Each time they began to wilt, the crowd, including us, would cheer them on. They made it to the end. I don't know how each of them would describe that experience from their adult perspectives, but I remember it as joyful. We snapped pictures to capture the day. These now-faded photos along with our memories would have been the only documentation of that singular time, if it weren't for what happened in phase three.

Two years later, in 1978, I was back in Wellfleet and roaming the art galleries. In one, there on the wall was a painting of the boys looking pretty much as I had captured them with my camera. I stood staring at the painting, not quite believing what was in front of me. It was magical. Philip was playing the fife, David banged the drum, and the young ones, bearing the flags, looked very fatigued. The artist told me that she had photographed the boys and decided to create what she thought was a charming slice of Americana. Several weeks later I brought my parents to view the painting but did not tell them what they were going to see. Just as I had, they stood in loving disbelief seeing the captured moment. My parents bought the painting, and now I have it displayed with one of the dim photographs of that day. Whenever my kids, nephews, and other family members visit they look at these items with wry smiles of understanding and memory.

The second painting and its accompanying story happened about twenty-five years later in 2000. Philip was now thirty-five and Daniel was thirty-two. The previous years had been full of achievement, but there were also trials. In 1999, my mother went into a nursing home and my aunt Lena died. It had been a very demanding time, and we all needed a vacation. We decided to take a trip together to a remote part of Belize to sit on a beach, do a little exploring, and drink piña coladas. We stayed at a slightly run-down resort. I think we were the only guests but it was warm, tropical, and stress-free. Somehow we learned that a local artist, Lola, had a studio nearby and we decided to visit. To get to Lola's place we walked down a dirt road until we came to a home-made arrow that showed the way—over a little rickety wooden bridge, through a hot and steamy swamp, and eventually to a little clearing with a few buildings. Lola and Eddie, her Rastafarian boyfriend, were there.

We looked at art and talked. Lola had a furious-looking swollen leg and Philip, who had recently completed his medical residency, examined it and gave Lola some advice. There was a lot of good fellowship, and Lola invited us to come back that evening for some rum punch and to learn punta dancing. Returning that night, the road was dark and the pathway into the swamp was eerie. I remember feeling wary but intrigued. When we arrived, Lola and Eddie were there, along with Lola's friend Martila and a small band of musicians—friends of Eddie's—who had come to play for us as we learned to dance. We danced, drank rum, and laughed a whole lot in the darkness, with only a few torches to light up the clearing.

Over the next few days, we saw Lola again, and we made a deal for her to do a painting of us in Belize. We may have even left a photograph for her to work from. A long time, maybe two years, went by without a painting, and then, one day it arrived. There we were with Lola, Martila, and Eddie. We were standing on a beach with blue sky and palm trees. The three of us looked somewhat like ourselves, along with Eddie who was skinny. But both Lola and Martila, who in real life were extremely large, had become slim and sexy. When Philip, Daniel, and I look at this painting, we have that same wry smile of understanding.

These two paintings hang in my house. They are of other times and disparate places. They each tell a story of a tiny slice of time and happenings. Up until now they have hung in different rooms, but I am going to put them opposite each other. I will be able to stand in between them and turn to one and remember my sons in childhood. Then I can turn to the other and remember them as adults. Many years elapsed between the creation of these two paintings, and a lot has happened with marriages, children, careers, and the family. Their lives and mine will continue to grow and change. So, I don't see the paintings as bookends to completed life chapters but more as reference points for reflection on my sons' and my life-stages. No matter what happens to each of us, the 1976 Wellfleet Fourth of July parade and the punta dancing in the Belize swamp will remain as important elements of a shared heritage, captured forever in two somewhat serendipitous but deeply evocative paintings.

…I am not interested in the abstract cogitation
any longer. I am interested in me.
I am a long way still from the fulfillment,
the total self-understanding that I long for now.
I remain a mystery to myself.
I want to get right down to the core,
make a final perfect equation before I am through,
balance it all up into a tidy *whole*.


— May Sarton, *As We Are Now*

# *My Places Within Myself: Mind and Body*

### The A List and the B List

### It's Never Too Late

### What's Fun?

### Walking and Talking

### Getting from Here to There

### Have You Prepared Yourself?

# The A List and the B List

MAKING DECISIONS IS a mixed bag for me. Sometimes it's easy because it is so clear what the right action should be, such as painting my peeling house or having my chimney relined. These choices were straightforward and uncomplicated because they involved basic, important elements of ordinary living. Harder decisions come when I haven't acknowledged that there are choices to be made.

About a year and a half ago, and a few days after I had been in the hospital for a minor health issue, my aunt Sylvia (who is herself aging in place) came to check on me. She is the last remaining relative of my parents' generation and is full of wisdom and good common sense. She drove herself to my house. We sat across from each other in my quiet living room and she asked how I was doing. I told her I was fine, taking it a little easy, and that all of me would be back to normal very soon—the rote response from someone who views herself as consummately independent. Then, with strong, precise clarity she said simply, "Marian, you do so many things. You must think about what you could give up in order to take some pressure off yourself! You have to make an A List and a B List."

I remember feeling a little stunned, being brought to sharp attention with no forewarning. "Why is she saying this to me?" I thought. "I am managing everything very well, thank you very much!" My work, children, grandchildren, community, friends, social life, writing…what's the big deal? I can do it all. Nothing I was doing had anything to do with this small health incident. I remember thanking her, figuring that I would probably ignore what she had said to me, believing I needed no advice. But that is not what happened.

Maybe it was because of my respect for her, or that a tiny part of me knew there could be some truth in her comments, but I took her words seriously. Looking back, I think that what really made me listen to Sylvia was the courage she showed in confronting the issue and challenging me directly—no hedging, no subtle hints, just straight observations. She did this in a matter-of-fact, no-nonsense, and above all, caring way, without a lot of emotional overlay. Her firm prodding made me stop and evaluate.

For several days, I thought about the A List/B List notion, and I concluded that it might have merit. There were many things that I did routinely, without stopping to think about either their worth to my existence or their potential for producing stress. What was I holding on to that I could gently let go? Initially, I put everything on the A List for one reason or another. Then I tried to imagine doing each item and whether I felt any anxiety when I carried it out. Sure enough, one thing popped up—my involvement with a choral group. I love to sing, always have. Growing up, it was something we all did in my family, and each time I sang as an adult it brought back lovely memories of my mother and father harmonizing to "Moonlight and Roses" in the kitchen. I thought about how it would feel not singing with the chorus that I had been involved with almost from its inception. Surprisingly, I felt relief at the idea of not having to rush to get to practice after my once-a-week day with my grandchildren (definitely the A List). Yes, I would miss the singing, but not the tension produced by trying to get there on time. So I stopped, and that has been quite all right. Someday maybe I'll go back, but only if I can find something to replace it on the B List.

This episode has given me some powerful and positive insights. First, I don't keep an active list of all of the things I do because my life keeps changing. Keeping a written record of what I do would be time-consuming, not to mention a bit neurotic (clearly something for the B List). But I find that each time priority-setting is called for I know I can create a new list and start the selection process all over again. Decisions are a bit easier and less scary because I know that an A List and a B List helps me be objective and lowers apprehension when I must make a choice. Second, I learned from Sylvia that being direct and caring is a good way to talk to the people I love about the challenges they may need to think about now and in the future. Most importantly, this way of thinking helps me to be in control of my own aging journey, at least for now. I don't have to be so afraid of upcoming decisions because I have a process that will help me see things more clearly.

Making an A List and a B List does take time, but it is worth the effort because it helps clarify the things that are most important. Like everything else, it's hard to get started, but it gets easier as you move through it, especially if you have a wise friend who can challenge you with kindness.

# It's Never Too Late

Every once in a while someone asks me to tell them the story about my going back to school at an "advanced" age. So maybe it is time that I actually wrote it down. Here it is.

My aunt Lena, with whom I was very connected, was my father's sister and the same age as my mother. Lena and my mom were sisters-in-law but also very good friends. Lena married late and never had any children, so over the years we became very close. Later in life, Lena asked me to be her health care proxy and power of attorney.

Lena lived to be 93 years old and loved every minute of her existence no matter how old and disabled she became. My uncle Eddie—my father's brother—was the baby of the family, and he too lived to be 93. My mom died at 95 and did pretty well until she was about 92. My mother's mother lived to be 86, and her parents lived to be 94 and 96. My dad died at 83. Other members on each side of the family failed to live to advanced ages, but nevertheless, I have a pretty good heritage of longevity on both sides of my family.

When I was about 63 years old I began to think about the likelihood that I too could have a pretty long life and wondered what I would do with those additional years—perhaps up to about 30. I knew that I wasn't the type to retire to some warm climate, at least at that point in my life. So, what's next now? I challenged myself to think about what things I would feel dissatisfied about if I didn't do them before age prevented me from starting. Surprisingly, it really didn't take long for me to decide; my top-priority item popped up immediately. Go back to school to get a Ph.D.—that was it! I had no doubts. Sure, I was a little worried about going back to school after so many years in light of the fact that I was never a great student. I was concerned about meeting my commitments to my family and close friends. Could I continue to work and earn enough money to support myself? No matter how many barriers I came up with, I simply set them aside. For whatever reason, I was totally convinced that I could do it. I figured I would work it out. In a way, it almost felt that I didn't have a choice.

In earlier years I had wanted to complete a doctorate after my master's degree, but ordinary life circumstances—moving, children, working, and inflexible academic rules—all stopped me from pursuing that final academic achievement. Without a lot of further thought I decided that it was time. "It's not too late," I kept telling myself. And it turned out I was right.

I applied to Antioch University New England; they accepted me, and I began the doctoral program shortly before my 64th birthday in 2002, with the goal of finishing by the time I was 70. In addition to being a student in those school years, I was a caregiver for my mother until she died in 2003; helped when I could with my uncle Eddie who had suffered a stroke; and took over chief responsibility for my disabled cousin Fred. Both of my kids got married (one in Japan); two of my three grandkids were born and I took care of them one day a week; I worked as a consultant not quite full-time but a lot; and I studied. When I look back I am not sure how I did it, but I never had any doubt that I would finish. My dissertation defense, which I passed in June 2008, was shortly before my 70th birthday.

People ask me if it was hard going back to school at an older age and I always respond, "Not really." In fact it was easier in many ways. I was a more focused and better student than I ever had been when I was younger. I plodded through the coursework and independent study, struggled with what my specific area of research should be, drafted and re-drafted essays and my dissertation, and worried that I wouldn't get through statistics given that I was an unparalleled math dummy.

What I learned was that I had more in me than I ever knew or acknowledged. My discoveries were that I could write; I had the confidence and maturity to be able to reject things that I deemed unimportant and could concentrate on what would get me closer to my goal; and I met wonderful people and it didn't matter that I was the oldest person in my cohort. We all learned from and respected each other.

As I think back on this now, I see that the stuff of ordinary existence—earning a living, taking care of loved ones, being there for my kids and grandkids—were going to happen no matter what else I did. Going back to school gave me the means and the strength to put all of that in a good perspective. It allowed me to take myself and my life goals seriously.

I tell people that pursuing this degree was one of the best things that I ever did. It wasn't the degree per se, but the fact that I successfully met and achieved my own challenge. It's not for everyone, this going back to school. But many of us have dreams both big and small. If we don't try to realize them, we may regret it. All I can say is that if something moves you, stirs your spirit, or sits out there as an unachieved goal—pay attention. It is never too late.

# What's Fun?

A number of people have suggested that I write something about having fun. Many of my articles are about hard issues, so this "fun" topic should have been a shift to something less weighty. It didn't turn out that way. I don't think I'm a downer-type person, but thinking about fun was perplexing and loaded with unexpected emotion. After many months, I figured out my two main quandaries: not knowing what fun was for me; and not understanding my reactions when someone asked me what I was doing for fun.

For the first question—what is *fun?*—I began in my usual way, with the dictionary. One definition says it is "enjoyment, amusement, or lighthearted pleasure." OK, there are many things that I enjoy, that amuse me, and in which I take pleasure. I'm fine with these ideas. But I have a little problem with the notion of "lighthearted." When I think of lighthearted the image that pops into my head is my junior prom dress—sweet, puffy, and aqua. I really loved that dress and still have a picture of me in it. I don't remember much about the prom, but I do remember having "lighthearted" feelings about the dress. That was close to sixty years ago. The dress is gone but I'm still here having accomplished a great deal since then. That lighthearted feeling may have been "fun" but it wasn't something that contributed greatly to my life over time. So a partial answer to the meaning of fun for me is that lightheartedness is good, but not as a standalone goal.

This sent me on a quest to figure out what fun is for me. I did this partly to convince myself that I am not an anomaly—a "funless" person. Also, I wanted to find a reasonable answer in response to questions about what I did for fun, one that was convincing. To do this I spent a lot of time talking to myself. No one but me knows how long and convoluted these inner discussions were.

I was never a big party-person, although I loved being with people, having a good time, sharing common experiences, singing, dancing, and laughing at jokes that at least we who were in the room thought were funny. I still do these things. What else has been fun for me? I love to travel to uncommon places. Those trips have been and will, I hope, continue to be fantastic. Going back to school was wonderful. It was hard work but I loved it (except statistics). We all agonized over the drudgery but had tremendous fun during our summer-session, Hawaiian-inspired, grass-skirted parties. I had a lot of fun with my kids when they were growing up (and still do), and now with my grandkids. I love going to theater, movies, opera, museums, or dinner with friends, but I also like doing these things by myself. Right now a lot of my fun revolves around writing. It's great when people tell me my articles hit home for them—it is enormously gratifying.

The other part of this "fun" thing is my reaction when asked what I do for fun. I feel oddly defensive, like I am supposed to be doing something more or better than what I already am. In my head, the question implies that there is some kind of lack in my life. I immediately begin to search my brain for an answer, but I get stuck right off the bat feeling bad and guilty. I don't have a good response. This is probably because I hadn't defined what "fun" meant for me. I have a better idea now.

My conclusion is that the abstract notion of fun doesn't have a lot of meaning. For me, fun must be embedded in a context of learning, communicating, contributing, or creating—my regular life. It is being with people I care about, sharing laughter, and, when necessary, sadness. It is being challenged. It is about seeing something work when it wasn't working before. This is my fun. Sometimes there is even lightheartedness—as in tropical island-themed revelries.

So, I have explained it to myself but what do I say to others without getting defensive? I guess the simplest thing to say is, "I am having fun with everything that I am doing." They may not understand, but I do, and that is really what matters most.

# Walking and Talking

I know I should exercise more and am aware of all the good reasons why: make my heart pump; keep my muscles strong; get rid of minor aches; and clear my mind. Exercise for me is primarily walking. I try to walk two or three times a week, mostly into the village or, when the weather is good, around Cold Spring Park. When I do get out and walk, I am proud that I am keeping myself healthy, and I feel the positive effects. But I am a lazy and reluctant exerciser. The congratulatory pats I give myself each time I walk are unwarranted because, if I am honest, I know that I may not walk again for days. When my doctor asks me how much I exercise, I lie and say I walk more than I do. Most of the time, I see myself as an honest mature thinker and decision-maker. When it comes to exercise, I am an inconsistent adolescent.

The reality is that I hate to get my body moving. It feels like an enormous effort to get motivated, dress properly, and take that first step out my back door. Why does it feel like such an oppressive task when it should be something to look forward to? Why can't I elevate the importance of this simple activity to something that becomes a life mission?

Maybe it is a physical thing. Ugh, that effort to move my bones and stir my arms and legs. It's not that my body is in bad shape (although that nagging arthritis in my neck is annoying and uncomfortable). It is more that it is very happy in a static state. It likes being holed up inert at home. "It's too hot, too cold, I'll walk tomorrow," I tell myself, and that gets me off the hook until the next day when I go through the same internal argument.

Maybe I avoid exercising because it is hard to see an immediate advantage. When I pay my bills, do the shopping, or finish an article, I get on-the-spot gratification. I procrastinate with these chores but they all have deadlines, and I know if I don't get them done, there will be consequences. But exercise is a different matter. The benefits seem down the road, disconnected, too far away in time for a sense of accomplishment. "In 20 years, will I be glad that I exercised when I was 72? Who cares?" I think. "And besides, my mother, who lived to be 95, never exercised much and look how old she got to be!"

When I do walk, I usually walk alone. A good part of me likes that solitude. In fact, that is one of the few things that pushes me out of the house—quiet time for reflection and talking to myself about current quandaries. There is immediate reward from my solitary walking—solutions to problems, getting rid of pent-up stress, or coming up with ideas for articles. But walking only when there is a mini-crisis brewing means it is haphazard.

I know I am missing something by walking by myself. I don't have the benefit of another voice to help me sort out what is going on in my head. Hearing another person's thoughts prompts me to think about things other than my own immediate issues. Each time I walk and talk with someone, I treasure their comments and find new ways of thinking. I love the back-and-forth creative exchange that only comes with quiet, intimate conversation. I admit it, I am stuck.

Seeking other ways to think about these issues, I talked to my city's Parks and Recreation programming director for the over 55 set. She reinforced, with passion, the importance of exercise for older people. "Being physically active is not about chasing after youth or trying to stay younger. It is about being healthy and independent as you get older. In fact, this can mean being able to live in your home longer." She described the out-of-door activities she manages and described three important aspects to all of them: exercising for a healthy body; learning new things; and staying socially connected. The last is a big incentive for people to join in. If I joined a walking group I would have lots of new people to talk to. The problem is I already have wonderful people to talk to, and I also like to talk to myself. But our program director is right when she says, "Not being physically active prevents you from moving forward. You can't change that you are getting older, but you do have some control over how you are going to arrive there!"

I know she is right and I take her advice quite seriously. But I am stuck on how to incorporate her wisdom into my daily life. In the meantime, I will continue to walk mostly alone and talk to myself. I will really, really try to become more physically active. Really! But I can't promise.

# Getting from Here to There

Lately, I have been thinking about how I get from one place to another. Those who plan systems for moving people around call it transportation. I, however, as an individual aging-in-placer, don't think "big" about "transportation"; I think "small" about how I can get from here to there. Usually, I go places with some specific goal in mind and, if I really planned it, I could probably get a lot of what I need by walking. I live .36 miles from a CVS where I can buy shampoo; .50 miles from the village where I can get a loaf of bread; and about 1.5 miles from the library. I also live .33 miles from the local train station, where I can catch a quick ride to many amenities. But I drive almost everywhere because it is easy, fast, and what I have become accustomed to as a resident of suburbia.

Underlying all of these getting-around musings are two profound and related issues. The first revolves around the complexity of my life. The second is about what will happen in the future if I cannot walk much or drive. I like to think about, and thoroughly delight in, my life's complexity, with its lush composition of family, friends, community, and culture. I do not like to think about not driving. Driving is the thing that keeps me connected to the multiple rich pieces of my being. It is a cornerstone for creating the milieu that best fits who I am and want to be. Thoughts about not driving create dread at the potential loss of connections to those pieces and, more importantly, dread at the loss of independence simply to be myself.

I can only speculate about this challenge because luckily I am still able to walk and drive. To really understand what happens to someone when these abilities become limited or end, I talked to my dear, longtime friend Susan, who I knew would be candid about what happened to her. "The realization that I had lost the body that I knew came gradually," she said. "For the first few months after the surgery, it didn't matter that I had to rely on other people. But after a while, I began to have that helpless feeling that I was stuck in a cage and the way out had been taken away from me."

Susan's husband was very willing to drive her places but she was loath to rely on him and others for simple things like picking up fruit, or getting a haircut. "I always considered myself an independent person. I could get in my car and do what I wanted—it was part of who I was. I was defined by my job, my good health, my physical activity. My independence was part of my strength. That is all gone. I slowly understood that the woman I used to be was not the person I am now. I am beginning to accept it, to live with it, but it feels rotten. Every morning I wake up thinking that it will be the way it was before, but it doesn't happen."

When Susan and I have dinner together after a movie, I still see the same person who is extraordinarily observant, has an astute sense of humor, and is passionate about societal issues. It doesn't matter how I experience being with her, though, it is how she feels about herself. "Yes," she said, "the basic person is still there, but those vital, defining peripheries of my life are getting smaller or disappearing. When you get older and have lost physical strength, you become dependent on others. You get used to it over time, but a part of my life has ended."

We suburbanites are particularly prone to this thorny aspect of aging in place. Ironically, we have set ourselves up to face a cruel dilemma. We moved to the suburbs to be away from the noisy city, raise our kids in a leafy environment, strive for upward mobility, and live in privacy within the walls of our separate homes. These elements are the underpinnings of the American-Dream notions of self-sufficiency and independence. However, this life-style also requires the ability to drive. Paradoxically, losing independence at an older age, and needing ways to get around other than driving ourselves, collides—sometimes abruptly—with our lifelong, ingrained perceptions of who we are as individuals and as a culture.

I do not have an answer to this dilemma, but getting older and losing physical capabilities will likely happen to most of us, albeit at different times in our aging process. A little anticipatory research might be a good thing to do. I can talk to friends, contact my local houses of worship, and find out what my local senior service agencies have to offer. Even if I don't need any help right now I have to be informed. It is one way for me to prepare for a future when I may have some trouble getting from here to there.

# Have You Prepared Yourself?

In early September of 2003 my mother had a stroke. She was already in a compromised condition, being 95 years old and wheelchair bound. She didn't look that frail. She was round and pink, but already past the time that she wanted to live. She was just waiting. Intellectually, I knew that she probably had only a little while longer but emotionally, unlike her, I wasn't ready.

In the days before the weekend when I was due to go to New Hampshire for my classes I was distracted and worried by what was going on. I wasn't even sure if I should leave, but the nursing home assured me that it was unlikely that something dire would happen over the next few days. I knew my mom was well taken care of, and with some nagging disquiet and guilt I decided to make the drive. Also, I had committed to hosting two women from the Lakota tribe in South Dakota who were to begin the graduate program where I had already completed one year of study. They were to stay at my house the night before and travel back and forth with me. When they arrived, I explained what was going on. They listened with great attention, expressed concern and understanding, but they did not say, "I hope she gets better," or "I hope things turn out all right." They asked, "Have you prepared yourself?" I was disconcerted by the question, never having been asked it before. In those few words they expressed a profound acceptance of what was ahead. There was no denying the inevitable outcome. Their probing question clearly and starkly laid the situation in front of me. My mom's future was her death and my future was to figure out how to face it.

I believe, now, that this potent question allowed me to begin the process of letting go. Up until then I had been holding on, doing everything that I could within reason (and within her wishes) to keep her alive and with me. I couldn't see that trying to sustain her life was less about her desires than my need to have her around. The question of preparing myself came at a critical moment. It forced me to recognize the obvious, which up until then, I had chosen to ignore. My mom was at the end of her life and I had to accept that. My job then became two-fold: be with her calmly until she died, and create a stepping-off point for moving my own life forward without her. This transition in thinking and acting didn't happen suddenly or dramatically. It occurred slowly over weeks as I gradually released her until she died a short time later.

From time to time over the nine years since then, I have considered this idea of preparing myself. I have found it useful to think about it related to many aspects of my life. I can ask: Have I prepared myself by making my wishes known to my children? Have I prepared myself for a decision to stay in my house or a move? Have I prepared myself for my financial needs? Have I prepared myself by having important papers in order? Have I prepared myself to accept dependence if I can't take care of myself anymore?

There is the risk of becoming obsessed with a list of all of the possible scenarios—something which feels less than healthy to me. Certainly there is no way to fully prepare for untoward events, but it feels quite positive to identify the key areas that could become problematic for me and perhaps place a burden on my kids. It offers a certain peace. By doing some thoughtful preparing I can take some time-consuming and guilt-filled guesswork out of my and my children's decision making. I am not only preparing myself; I am preparing them.

Along with all of the rational commonsense explanations for asking this question there is something more profound. I, like so many of us, don't want to think about what may happen. I don't want to think about losing my independence and control. I don't want to face so many, many things. And hopefully I won't have to. But the idea of preparing myself creates a new perspective. It gives me permission to think about my life in a different way, one based on reality, not on fear of the unknown—a fear that can trap me and my family in a false sense of permanence. It is freeing, enlightening. It is a more thoughtful way of dealing with thorny issues for now and in the future. Most importantly, it gives me the power to deny the denial, and it allows me to exert my independence as a mature, competent older adult.

Time

is divided into two rivers:

one

flows backward, devouring

life already lived;

the other

moves forward with you

exposing

your life.

For a single second

they may be joined.

Now.

This is that moment,

the drop of an instant

that washes away the past.

It is the present.

It is in your hands.


— Pablo Neruda, "Ode to the Past,"
    *Selected Odes of Pablo Neruda*

# *Future Focus*

# Future Focus

WITH THESE ESSAYS, I have laid down some of my thoughts about what it is like to get older. My writing is from my expansive experience and endless reflections on who I am as an aging person: a daughter, mother, grandmother, friend, and caregiver, combined with being a member of several "communities" and society at large. My goal has been to capture my personal reactions to how I am linked to all of my "places" in a way that feels honest to me. Hopefully, my thoughts will seem familiar to others and they will benefit in some way from my words.

I have come a long way in achieving this goal, and I will likely continue to think and write down my experiences for many years to come. However, it would be so easy to observe and record what is going on inside and outside me, and then lazily sit back, thinking that my job is done just because I composed some words. If I wanted to leave it at this point, I could just conclude by saying such things as "these are my reflections, I hope they resonate with you, and good luck in thinking about your own future." But although I am writing about my innermost self, what I have said so far seems, in an odd way, detached and somewhat bookish.

This isn't enough, at least for me. It would feel an incomplete, unproductive, and unsatisfying effort if, after doing all of this reflective work, I didn't consider how to use my understanding to inform some meaningful next steps for myself. This part has been hard. For a while now I have wondered why, with all of my experience living life, I find it really difficult and daunting to apply what I know, so intimately and deeply, to what I must do for myself for my own future. Without question, it is tough to think about the concept of a future, probably because whatever time is left to me is so uncertain, as it is for everyone. As a younger person I planned for getting educated and achieving independence, for raising a family, for finding jobs to support myself, and for maintaining a stable life. There was a degree of certainty and necessity about this path, which defined the tasks in order to remain focused enough to get through the next day, week, year, or decade.

But things are quite different now and perhaps less clear because I don't know what challenges and dilemmas I will face. However, this uncertainty doesn't get me off the hook for continuing to plan. The most productive way for me to approach this challenge is to create two categories of goals: one concrete, with defined end points; and the other, ongoing activities that are important to me. Concrete goals, such as writing another book, create a tangible image of things to accomplish and can be excellent motivators to keep moving ahead. The other category includes what I do every day, such as staying connected with friends or making contributions to my community.

So, I need to do a little planning. My experience tells me that it is better to do that sooner rather than later. I know that if there are no plans it is easy to float along without purpose, leaving to chance what happens each day. But it is tricky to think about the "how" without a good model to rely on that goes beyond repetitious and hackneyed admonitions to stay healthy, active, and engaged. Since a satisfactory paradigm (at least one that works for me) doesn't exist, I've created my own. Perhaps by designing and then using this paradigm it will make setting and achieving goals a bit easier.

This is where the notion of "places" can be very useful. The idea of places makes less opaque the process of determining where to focus decision making. Using a framework of the "places" with which I interact can help me focus on the arenas that are most important to me, and what my role, desires, and interactions could be within each place. As I go along I can broaden or cut back on these places, depending on how I want to contemplate and live my life. What I don't know I can find out about. I just need a few telephone numbers or websites. Ultimately, the responsibility for figuring this out and acting on it is mine. I need to be the information gatherer and distiller about things that have to do with me. I have to work on my own behalf to identify what I need, find out where it is, and if it is not available, be my own advocate and activist to get it. I also must figure out where I can contribute my skills and knowledge in a way that has meaning for others.

Taking a few steps upward I see that just having the framework and the list of places still isn't enough. I need to know how this fits into some overall vision and mission for my complex life. Basically, I need a strategic plan. As I understand it, a strategic plan involves having a vision (what the ideal state might look like from 500 feet); having a mission (the things that would help achieve that vision); and having some strategic goals with steps that would help make the vision and mission a reality.

# My Vision

My vision must be realistic and doable. I acknowledge the possibility that unexpected things can happen. My vision gathers together my wishes for my life into the future and has the capacity to guide all decisions.

I close my eyes and envision what I want my life to look like going forward. These elements are important to the realization of my vision.

- I define what is meaningful to me—not according to someone else's goals.

- I have people around me whom I care about and who care about me.

- I contribute in good, constructive ways to family, friends, and society.

- People benefit from knowing me and I from knowing them.

- I am at peace with my life and goals.

# My Mission

My mission defines my values, roles, and responsibilities in carrying out my vision. It helps me know what I need to do to make my vision a reality. These elements are important to the realization of my mission. By doing all of this I serve myself, my loved ones, and the communities of which I am a part.

- I am the leader and organizer of my life until I can no longer function physically, but more importantly, intellectually and emotionally.
- Others contribute collaboratively to help me achieve my vision.
- I keep myself physically and mentally healthy and engaged.
- I make decisions consistent with my vision and consider the impact on others.
- I use my skills and knowledge wisely.
- I help others to the best of my ability.
- I trust those whom I have designated as my decision-makers.

# My Strategic Goals

My goals outline specific areas to work on in order to achieve my vision and mission for the immediate and longer-term future. These goals are placed within the framework of the "places" I inhabit and where I function. In creating your own goals, you can use this framework, or feel free to create your own.

- *My Society and Culture*
  **Goal:** To advocate for a worldview that sees older people as community assets and acknowledges their contributions to culture and society, while understanding their true needs.

- *My Natural World*
  **Goal:** To treat the natural world with respect and kindness so that I and others can continue to learn from it and find peace within it.

- *My Community and Neighborhood*
  **Goal:** To help build communities and neighborhoods that value older adults, engage them in meaningful community contributions, and assist them as they age in places they choose.

- *My House*
  **Goal:** To live in a place that is consistent with and supports my lifestyle in keeping with my personal values and financial resources.

- *My Family and Friends*
  **Goal:** To enhance connections and contribute positively to family, as well as to older and newer friends.

- *My Mind and My Body*

  **Goal:** To maintain my mind and body to the best extent possible so that they continue to contribute to a positive future.

Each of these goals requires further effort to identify the specific actions I need to take to achieve them. It is a relief to have a framework that can help me move forward. It makes it harder for me to deny what can happen in the future and lets me know that the paths I create for myself don't have to be daunting or fraught with fear or anxiety. I can see the steps that are directly in front of me. They are not mysteries but quite clear, and they can be as simple or complex as I make them. Most importantly, I must assume that I have a future, and I must be diligent to plan for it.

# Sample Strategic Goal: Society and Culture

| | |
|---|---|
| *Place:* | My Society and Culture |
| *Strategic goal:* | To advocate for a worldview that sees older people as community assets and acknowledges their contributions to culture and society, while understanding true needs. |
| *Specific task:* | Bring my voice as a competent older adult into a public forum. |
| *My options?* | • Write column for local newspaper<br><br>• Make presentations<br><br>• Join advocacy group<br><br>• Write a book |
| *Bottom-line issues for me?* | • Ageism exists in our society<br><br>• Older people are not seen as valuable resources<br><br>• Older people don't have a voice from their perspective<br><br>• Denial of aging is unproductive and perilous |
| *My wishes?* | • Reduce ageist perceptions<br><br>• Older people are empowered to be self-advocates<br><br>• Older people know that many experience same dilemma |

| | |
|---|---|
| *Realistic?* | • Act locally<br>• Don't know about nationally<br>• Need to keep working |
| *Alternative plan?* | • Don't have one<br>• Need to keep talking and writing |
| *Information needed?* | • Perceptions of aging from various disciplines<br>• What others are doing to influence cultural perceptions<br>• Baby Boomer perceptions |
| *Informational resources?* | • AARP<br>• University research<br>• Other senior advocacy groups |
| *Next steps?* | • Keep writing and talking<br>• Get book published<br>• Search university research efforts<br>• Find someone to collaborate with |
| *Timing?* | • Now, until I can't do it any more |

# Sample Strategic Goal: House

| | |
|---|---|
| *Place:* | My House |
| *Strategic goal:* | To live in a place that is consistent with and supports my lifestyle in keeping with my personal values and financial resources. |
| *Specific task:* | Where should I live as I get older? |
| *My options?* | • Apartment (condo or rental)<br><br>• Stay in my house with support<br><br>• Continuing care community<br><br>• Assisted living<br><br>• Nursing home |
| *Bottom-line issues for me?* | • Safety<br><br>• Not isolated/socially connected<br><br>• Mentally/physically encouraged<br><br>• Near family<br><br>• Least burden on family/friends<br><br>• Affordability |
| *My wishes?* | • Stay in same community<br><br>• Rental or condo apartment<br><br>• Near public transportation |
| *Realistic?* | • What are rental/condo options in community?<br><br>• How much could I sell my house for? |
| *Alternative plan?* | • Stay in my house with support |

| Information needed? | • What exists in the area?<br>• What exists outside the area?<br>• Assess physical and mental status<br>• Assess financial status |
|---|---|
| Informational resources? | • Senior Center/Council on Aging<br>• State AARP<br>• State Elder Affairs<br>• Word of mouth<br>• Fee-for-service housing consultant |
| Next steps? | • Gather information |
| Timing? | • Make a decision in next two years |

# My Strategic Goal: _____

| | |
|---|---|
| *Place:* | |
| *Strategic goal:* | |
| *Specific task:* | |
| *My options?* | |
| *Bottom-line issues for me?* | |
| *My wishes?* | |
| *Realistic?* | |
| *Alternative plan?* | |
| *Information needed?* | |
| *Informational resources?* | |
| *Next steps?* | |
| *Timing?* | |

# Resources

This is not an exhaustive list but includes books that I have found helpful, challenging, and at times inspirational in considering the nature of my life and the places in which I am aging.

## General

Carstensen, Laura L. *A Long Bright Future: An Action Plan for a Lifetime of Happiness, Health, and Financial Security.* New York: Broadway Books, 2009.

Chopra, Deepak. *Ageless Body, Timeless Mind: The Quantum Alternative to Growing Old.* New York: Harmony Books, 1993.

Cole, Thomas R. *The Journey of Life: A Cultural History of Aging in America.* Canto ed. New York: Cambridge University Press, 1997.

Hanh, Thich Nhat. *Peace Is Every Step: The Path of Mindfulness in Everyday Life.* New York: Bantam Books, 1992.

Knapp, Marian Leah Gilbert. "Aging in Place in Suburbia: A Qualitative Study of Older Women." Ph.D. diss. Antioch University New England, 2009.

Vaillant, George E. *Aging Well: Surprising Guideposts to a Happier Life from the Landmark Harvard Study of Adult Development.* Boston: Little, Brown and Company, 2002.

## Place

Bachelard, Gaston. *The Poetics of Space.* (Original work published 1958.) Boston: Beacon Press, 1994.

Cresswell, Tim. *In Place/Out of Place: Geography, Ideology, and Transgression.* Minneapolis: University of Minnesota Press, 1996.

Cresswell, Tim. *Place: A Short Introduction.* Oxford, UK: Blackwell Publishing Ltd., 2004.

Lefebvre, Henri. *The Production of Space.* Oxford, UK: Blackwell Publishing Ltd., 1991.

Tuan, Yi-Fu. *Space and Place: The Perspective of Experience.* Minneapolis: University of Minnesota Press, 1977.

## Suburbs

Baxandall, Rosalyn, and Elizabeth Ewen. *Picture Windows: How the Suburbs Happened.* New York: Basic Books, 2000.

Bogosian, Eric. *Suburbia.* New York: Theatre Communications Group, Inc., 2004.

Duany, Andres, Elizabeth Plater-Zyberk, and Jeff Speck. *Suburban Nation: The Rise and Sprawl and the Decline of the American Dream.* New York: North Point Press, 2000.

Dunham-Jones, Ellen, and June Williamson. *Retrofitting Suburbia: Urban Design Solutions for Redesigning Suburbs.* Hoboken: John Wiley & Sons, Inc., 2011.

Hayden, Dolores. *Building Suburbia: Green Fields and Urban Growth, 1820–2000.* New York: Vintage Books, 2004.

Owens, Bill. *Suburbia.* New York: Fotofolio, Inc., 1999.

## American Dream

Cullen, Jim. *The American Dream: A Short History of an Idea That Shaped a Nation.* New York: Oxford University Press, 2003.

Jillson, Calvin C. *Pursuing the American Dream: Opportunity and Exclusion Over Four Centuries.* Lawrence: University Press of Kansas, 2004.

Samuel, Lawrence R. *The American Dream: A Cultural History.* Syracuse: Syracuse University Press, 2012.

## Society and Culture

Atwood, Margaret. *The Blind Assassin.* New York: Anchor Books, 2001.

Fischer, David Hackett. *Growing Old in America: The Bland-Lee Lectures Delivered at Clark University.* Expanded ed. New York: Oxford University Press, 1978.

Gillick, Muriel R. *The Denial of Aging: Perpetual Youth, Eternal Life, and Other Dangerous Fantasies.* Cambridge, MA: Harvard University Press, 2006.

Gullette, Margaret Morganroth. *Aged by Culture.* Chicago: University of Chicago Press, 2004.

Gullette, Margaret Morganroth. *Agewise: Fighting the New Ageism in America.* Chicago: University of Chicago Press, 2011.

Myerhoff, Barbara. *Number Our Days.* New York: Touchstone/Simon & Schuster, Inc., 1980.

Rosofsky, Ira. *Nasty, Brutish, and Long: Adventures in Old Age and the World of Eldercare.* New York: Penguin Group, 2009.

Sarton, May. *As We Are Now.* New York: W. W. Norton & Company, 1982.

## Natural World

Glyck, Vivian Elisabeth. *12 Lessons on Life I Learned from My Garden.* Emmaus, PA: Daybreak/Rodale Press, Inc., 1997.

Thoreau, Henry David. *Walden: Or Life in the Woods.* Reprint ed. Radford, VA: Wilder Publications, LLC., 2008.

Wessels, Tom. *Reading the Forested Landscape: A Natural History of New England.* Woodstock, VT: Countryman Press, 1999.

Williams, Terry Tempest. *Refuge: An Unnatural History of Family and Place.* New York: Vintage Books, 2001.

## Community and Neighborhood

Abbott, Pauline S., Nancy Carman, Jack Carman, and Bob Scarfo. *Re-creating Neighborhoods for Successful Aging.* Baltimore: Health Professions Press, 2009.

Block, Peter. *Community: The Structure of Belonging.* San Francisco: Berrett-Koehler Publishers, Inc., 2008.

Coles, Robert. *The Call of Service: A Witness to Idealism.* New York: Houghton Mifflin Harcourt, 1994.

Kretzmann, John P., and John L. McKnight. *Building Communities from the Inside Out: A Path Toward Finding and Mobilizing a Community's Assets.* Chicago: ACTA Publications, 1993.

McKnight, John L., and Peter Block. *The Abundant Community: Awakening the Power of Families and Neighborhoods.* San Francisco: Berrett-Koehler Publishers, Inc., 2010.

Putnam, Robert D. *Bowling Alone: The Collapse and Revival of American Community.* New York: Simon & Schuster Paperbacks, 2000.

## House and Home

Cooper Marcus, Clare. *House as a Mirror of Self: Exploring the Deeper Meaning of Home.* Berkeley, CA: Conari Press, 1997.

Heathcote, Edwin. *The Meaning of Home.* London: Frances Lincoln, 2012.

Stafford, Philip B. *Elderburbia: Aging with a Sense of Place in America.* Westport, CT: Praeger, 2009.

## Family and Friends

Arrison, Sonia. *100 Plus: How the Coming Age of Longevity Will Change Everything, from Careers and Relationships to Family and Faith.* New York: Basic Books, 2011.

Gross, Jane. *A Bittersweet Season: Caring for Our Aging Parents—and Ourselves.* New York: Alfred A. Knopf, 2011.

Menaker, Daniel. *Friends and Relations: A Collection of Stories.* Garden City, New York: Doubleday, 1976.

Span, Paula. *When the Time Comes: Families with Aging Parents Share Their Struggles and Solutions.* New York: Springboard Press, 2009.

## Mind and Body

Baltes, Paul B., and Margret M. Baltes. *Successful Aging: Perspectives from the Behavioral Sciences.* Cambridge, UK: Cambridge University Press, 1993.

Buettner, Dan. *The Blue Zones: Lessons for Living Longer from the People Who've Lived the Longest.* Washington, DC: National Geographic Society, 2008.

Cohen, Gene D. *The Mature Mind: The Positive Power of the Aging Brain.* New York: Basic Books, 2006.

Cozolino, Louis. *The Healthy Aging Brain: Sustaining Attachment, Attaining Wisdom.* New York: W. W. Norton & Company, 2008.

Loe, Meika. *Aging Our Way: Lessons for Living from 85 and Beyond.* New York: Oxford University Press, 2011.

Rowe, John W., and Robert L. Kahn. *Successful Aging.* New York: Random House Large Print, 1998.

Sarton, May. *As We Are Now.* New York: W. W. Norton & Company, 1992.

Strauch, Barbara. *The Secret Life of the Grown-Up Brain: The Surprising Talents of the Middle-Aged Mind.* New York: Viking/Penguin, 2010.

## Chapter Heading Quotations

Atwood, Margaret. *The Blind Assassin.* New York: Anchor Books, 2001, (p. 43).

Cohen, Gene. *The Mature Mind: The Positive Power of the Aging Brain.* New York: Basic Books, 2006, (p. xiii).

Cresswell, Tim. *In Place/Out of Place: Geography, Ideology and Transgression*. Minneapolis: University of Minnesota Press, 1996, (p. 13).

Eliade, Mircea. *The Sacred and the Profane: The Nature of Religion*. Orlando: Harcourt, Inc., 1987, (p. 56).

Neruda, Pablo. From *Selected Odes of Pablo Neruda, Translated, with Introduction by Margaret Sayers Peden*. "Ode to the Past". Berkeley: University of California Press, 1990, (pp. 114–115).

Putnam, Robert D. *Bowling Alone: The Collapse and Revival of American Community*. New York: Simon & Schuster Paperbacks, 2000, (pp. 273–274).

Sarton, May. *As We Are Now*. New York: W. W. Norton & Company, 1992, Reissue ed., (p. 24).

Wessels, Tom. *Reading the Forested Landscape: A Natural History of New England*. Woodstock, VT: The Countryman Press, 1999, (p. 165).

Dr. Knapp is available for speaking engagements, lectures, hands-on workshops, interviews, and book signings. She can be reached at marianlknapp@gmail.com.